NEW DIRECTIONS FOR HIGHER EDUCATION

Martin Kramer
EDITOR-IN-CHIEF

How Accreditation Influences Assessment

James L. Ratcliff, Edward S. Lubinescu,
Maureen A. Gaffney
Pennsylvania State University

EDITORS

Number 113, Spring 2001

JOSSEY-BASS
San Francisco

How Accreditation Influences Assessment
James L. Ratcliff, Edward S. Lubinescu, Maureen A. Gaffney (eds.)
New Directions for Higher Education, no. 113
Martin Kramer, Editor-in-Chief

Microfilm copies of issues and articles are available in 16mm and 35mm, as well as microfiche in 105mm, through University Microfilms Inc., 300 North Zeeb Road, Ann Arbor, Michigan 48106-1346.

ISSN 0271-0560   ISBN 0-7879-5436-5

New Directions for Higher Education is part of The Jossey-Bass Higher and Adult Education Series and is published quarterly by Jossey-Bass Inc., 350 Sansome Street, San Francisco, California 94104-1342. Periodicals postage paid at San Francisco, California, and at additional mailing offices. Postmaster: Send address changes to New Directions for Higher Education, Jossey-Bass Inc., 350 Sansome Street, San Francisco, California 94104-1342.

Subscriptions cost $59 for individuals and $114 for institutions, agencies, and libraries. See Ordering Information page at end of book.

Editorial correspondence should be sent to the Editor-in-Chief, Martin Kramer, 2807 Shasta Road, Berkeley, California 94708-2011.

Cover photograph and random dot by Richard Blair/Color & Light © 1990.

Jossey-Bass Web address: www.josseybass.com

CONTENTS

EDITORS' NOTES

Accreditation and student learning outcomes have been discussed extensively throughout the literature on higher education. This literature provides information and evidence depicting the issues, concerns, and effective practices within both processes. Yet surprisingly, both accreditation and assessment are only weakly understood by many charged with carrying them out on campuses. With the increasing need to demonstrate student learning outcomes as a part of institutional and programmatic requirements, questions and concerns are naturally raised about how the two processes fit together and what can be done to ensure an optimal fit.

This volume, *How Accreditation Influences Assessment,* is about making the connection between the assessment of student learning outcomes and both regional and programmatic accreditation. We have sought to provide a balance of perspectives on regional and programmatic accreditation and include the viewpoints of accrediting agency officials, campus leaders involved with accreditation and assessment, and higher education researchers. Two questions unify the chapters: (1) How should student learning outcomes be demonstrated in the accreditation process? and (2) How should assessment information be used to show improvement in programs, services, and student learning?

Chapter One provides an introduction for those seeking basic information on accreditation and assessment: what they are, why they exist, how they work, and who is responsible. Here we set out what by necessity must be only an initial review of the background and underlying issues affecting regional accreditation, programmatic accreditation, and student learning outcomes. This chapter provides a framework for those that follow, allowing a grasp of the basic issues and providing conclusions about the interconnections between accreditation and student learning outcomes assessment.

In Chapter Two, Susan R. Hatfield describes how the shift of accreditation from standards to student outcomes requires defining the best way to measure the benefits that students are receiving from their education. Hatfield demonstrates that student academic achievement is best assessed at the department or program level. She analyzes the factors involved in conducting a self-study, including setting goals, facilitating outcomes, and choosing specific types of outcomes. The concepts of formative and summative evaluation, quantitative and qualitative methodologies, and individual and holistic outcomes guide her discussion.

In the past decade, there has been great concern over the role of accreditation and student learning outcomes with relation to distance education. In Chapter Three, Watson Scott Swail and Eva Kampits discuss the rise of distance education, the challenges to traditional higher education, and how to maintain quality accreditation and assessment standards in the new medium. They focus on how to introduce accreditation resources and processes in such a way as to respond to the need for quality assurance. Their examples and recommendations provide a comprehensive outline of the issues and concerns regarding accreditation, assessment, and distance education.

For some time, there has been a need to evaluate the purposes of procedural and substantive standards and their role in evaluating learning outcomes. In Chapter Four, Frank Brush Murray addresses this concern. Using the example of teacher education, he explores in depth how the procedural and consensus standards of accrediting agencies may not be providing enough evidence that student learning is occurring. He argues that other lines of evidence can be used as well to understand various aspects of an educator's competence: input from independent assessments, the states, school boards, professional societies, and the public. He claims that these lines of evidence need to be grounded in scholarly and professional literature, as well as the standards of scholarship.

Throughout the history of accreditation and student learning outcomes assessment, standards have been set to evaluate whether institutions and programs are meeting the desired expectations of their accrediting bodies and state mandates. With increasing emphasis being placed on the shared responsibility of assessing student learning outcomes, there is some concern over how often standards should change. In Chapter Five, Cynthia A. Davenport examines this concern through a survey and review of more than twenty written accreditation policies. She argues that standards should be responsive without placing heavy regulatory burdens on institutions and accrediting agencies.

In Chapter Six, we turn attention from agency to institution. Kathi A. Ketcheson examines the role of public accountability and reporting in the self-study process. Through her study of the Urban Universities Portfolio Project, Ketcheson examines the issues and concerns that need to be addressed when considering what aspects of accreditation and student learning outcomes assessment should be available to the public. She comprehensively reviews both the successes and failures of instituting an electronic portfolio as a method for documenting institutional accountability and performance.

In the concluding chapter, Rebecca R. Martin, Kathleen Manning, and Judith A. Ramaley discuss how an institutional accreditation self-study was used as a means for instilling a strategic change process at the University of Vermont. This case study presents valuable insights on how to involve faculty, staff, and students in the accreditation process. The authors argue that accreditation can be built on the strengths of both administrative and faculty culture. Through the detail they provide, they communicate an effective way to implement an institutional self-study as a vehicle of change.

Although the arenas in which assessment and accreditation intersect are numerous today, this volume highlights six salient new directions that together offer insight into ways that student, faculty, and institutional learning can be enhanced through the accreditation process and how that learning can be transformative to the programs, services, and systems found within our colleges and universities.

Edward S. Lubinescu
James L. Ratcliff
Maureen A. Gaffney
Editors

EDWARD S. LUBINESCU is a doctoral candidate and graduate research assistant at the Shreyer Institute for Teaching and Learning, Pennsylvania State University.

JAMES L. RATCLIFF is president of Performance Associates Postsecondary Consulting in Pueblo, Colorado and is affiliate senior scientist and former director of the Center for the Study of Higher Education at Pennsylvania State University.

MAUREEN A. GAFFNEY is a doctoral candidate and graduate research assistant in higher education at Pennsylvania State University.

1

The accountability movement in the 1990s that followed the campus-based assessment movement of the 1980s produced the link between accreditation and student outcomes assessment. Two parallel continuums can be seen: one detailing the cycle of accreditation and the other student outcomes assessment. Now the two continuums have merged.

Two Continuums Collide: Accreditation and Assessment

Edward S. Lubinescu, James L. Ratcliff, Maureen A. Gaffney

Calls for accountability and improvement reverberate with higher education's internal and external constituencies today. The dialogue takes a variety of forms: cost and benefit, implementation of on-line learning, greater engagement with the communities the institution serves, program renewal, organizational transformation, and changing the accreditation process itself. Yet stakeholders have found common ground in the discussions and concerns focused on student learning outcomes. Increasingly they are becoming embedded in the accrediting process in a variety of ways. Regardless of whether the accreditation is programmatic, institutional, or virtual, colleges and universities are expected to show effective student learning outcomes. The Council for Higher Education Accreditation (CHEA), the body that brings together the various forms of higher education accreditation in the United States, recognizes the obligation that institutions and the accrediting bodies have in addressing continuing public pressure for evidence of student learning outcomes (Eggers, 2000).

Accreditation and student learning outcomes assessment have been discussed extensively. This volume examines contemporary dimensions of how accreditation and student outcomes assessment come together. Running through the dimensions explored in this volume are two key questions:

- How should student learning outcomes be demonstrated in the accreditation process?
- How should assessment information be used to show improvement in programs, services, and student learning?

NEW DIRECTIONS FOR HIGHER EDUCATION, no. 113, Spring 2001 © Jossey-Bass, A Publishing Unit of John Wiley & Sons, Inc.   5

In our discussions with faculty serving on self-study teams and with college administrators overseeing accreditation processes, we find that many
involved do not reflect on or fully understand what accreditation is, what ends
it serves, and what its connection to the assessment of student learning may
be. This chapter thus provides a backdrop for the discussions that follow.

Accreditation Purposes and Processes

Accreditation may be "the most fully developed institutionalization of the
idea of accountability in higher education" (van Vught, 1994, p. 42). Within
the context of the United States, accreditation has the following purposes:

Fostering excellence through the development of criteria and guidelines for
    assessing effectiveness
Encouraging improvement through ongoing self-study and planning
Ensuring external constituents that a program has clearly defined goals and
    appropriate objectives, maintains faculty and facilities to attain them,
    demonstrates it is accomplishing them, and has the prospect for contin-
    uing to do so
Provides advice and counsel to new and established programs in the accred-
    iting process
Ensures that programs receive sufficient support and are free from external
    influence that may impede their effectiveness and their freedom of inquiry

In the United States, regional bodies accredit institutions of higher education. These have separate and different standards and guidelines from program accrediting agencies (Ratcliff, 1998). Whereas a program review may
serve as a basis for reallocation of resources toward a specific program, the
institutional accreditation assists in achieving a balance of human and financial resources among the various programs.

Van Vught (1994) has presented a vision of a multidimensional system
of accreditation wherein a number of accrediting organizations coexist, each
using its own standards, guidelines, and review processes. These different
accrediting bodies represent different constituencies external to the program
and the university. Some serve to attest to institutional, program, or student
quality to the government, while others may represent the needs and views
of employers, students, or the specific field of study. Taken together, they
provide multiple frames of reference in determining the quality of the institution, the program, and the student experience, forming a "market" in
which institutions of higher education "compete" for students, research
awards, and public recognition. In such a system, governments clearly have
the right and responsibility to decide what constitutes an accrediting body.
Governments may also wish to review accrediting procedures to ensure that
there are adequate procedural safeguards and rigorous application of program standards. In such a vision, the accrediting body becomes a meta-level

agent to the field of study, and the government makes procedural rather than substantive specification of the quality review process (Ratcliff, 1998).

What are the elements of a multidimensional system of evaluation that incorporates the evaluation of institutions, programs, and students? First, there needs to be a managing body that is legally empowered to recognize programs deemed legitimate and efficacious. This is the accrediting association, agency, or organization, which is most often empowered by the state and recognized by the federal government to determine quality for programs or institutions. Second, academics of the field need to have a substantive involvement in the development of standards and guidelines for conducting accreditation program reviews so that they may bear the credence desired with internal and external constituencies. Third, the process needs to provide for mechanisms by which a faculty of the program under review accepts the team of external peers assigned to the review process. If the team does not have the confidence of the faculty, it likely will not be persuasive in presenting its findings and recommendations. Fourth, the report of the site visitation team should be developed according to guidelines by which the process is approached as one of communication. That is, the utility of the evaluation of program strengths and weakness and of any recommendations or suggestions made by the site review team is diminished to the extent that it is not fully understood and deliberated by the program faculty and host institution. Fifth, the relationship between the program review process and the funding process needs to be clearly articulated. If funding decisions and the review are tied, then there need to be clear criteria to determine at what point a weak program will receive enhancements or be subject to discontinuance. Several writers in the field of quality assurance believe it best to separate funding and review processes rather than to link them tightly (Barak, 1982; George, 1982; van Vught and Westerheijden, 1993).

The accreditation process has at least five steps (Kells, 1992, p. 32):

1. The accrediting body sets standards, produces guidelines, and often provides training to peers in the program review process.
2. The program describes its goals and objectives, its faculty, facilities, and courses of study, and evaluates its strengths and weaknesses relative to its goals.
3. An evaluation team of peers identified by the accrediting body visits the program, using the guidelines and standards to examine faculty, facilities, students, and administrators. The team provides oral commentary followed by a written report to the accrediting body and to the institution housing the program under review.
4. The institution and its faculty respond to the report, providing supplemental evidence where questions remain, and indicating if and where they take exception with the findings of the report.
5. The accrediting body decides to grant, reaffirm, or deny accreditation to the program based on the self-study, the visiting team's findings, and the

institutional reply. Frequently accreditation is reaffirmed with the accrediting body making specific recommendations or suggestions for improvement during the forthcoming accrediting period.

Program (or Specialized) Accreditation. Program accreditation, a quality assurance process based on program review, is a means to verify the quality of academic programs and of institutions to external stakeholders. The accreditation process most often involves a formal review, with self-study of a specific academic program, evaluations by peers and external constituents, and a report to the agency, association, or organization that will certify program quality. The accrediting process necessarily encompasses the judgment of peers, as well as some determination of the extent to which the program is needed—through formal needs assessment—or valued—through graduate follow-up or employer surveys. An external body judges the quality of the program using clearly defined standards for the review and a process of self-study where the program's goals and their fulfillment are judged according to the accrediting body's standards. Accrediting bodies assemble a group of peers to review the self-study report, conduct site visits, and render judgments used in the accrediting process (Young and others, 1983). However, there are no established bases for determining who are the relevant external stakeholders, how they are selected, and what program information should guide their judgment about program effectiveness.

Accreditation needs to fulfill two dimensions of program quality. First, there should be some evidence that the programs have clear goals and courses of study to attain them. Second, the process should demonstrate that responsibilities associated with the goals are being carried out (Ewell, 1987). For a typical academic program, it means showing that the program provides courses of study appropriate to the disciplinary field, conducts research in the bodies of knowledge within its purview, and engages in service activities appropriate to the university and the field. It is also increasingly incumbent on the program to portray its impact on students, the discipline and the advance of knowledge within it, and the university and the communities it serves.

In program accreditation, peers interpret quality within the context of the program's own aims and activities. Central to specialized accreditation is the program review conducted as a self-study process. The underlying assumption of the self-study is that evaluators from outside the field of study cannot credibly or effectively examine the quality of a program in depth unless those carrying out the program have first studied and reached a judgment about its quality (Kells, 1992).

Institutional (or Regional) Accreditation. Regional accreditation can be defined as "a quality assurance process based on the voluntary association of schools and colleges" (Ratcliff, 1996). As defined by the CHEA (1996), certain defining characteristics are symbolic of the regional accreditation process. Regional accreditation:

1. Is a process in which a set of criteria is used to evaluate the effectiveness of an institution
2. Is voluntary and is not required by the state or federal government
3. Is a process that reflects the mission, history, and purpose of an institution
4. Is a process that presents evidence to external constituents that an institution meets or surpasses the criteria used in the evaluation
5. Does not normally use comparison in its methods; rather, it treats each institution as a unique entity
6. Is orchestrated by an external, voluntary commission comprised of representatives from the region
7. Is a process wherein the involvement of faculty and staff is regarded as fundamental to its legitimacy
8. Is conducted each time on the basis of a typical ten-year time period
9. Is a process that acknowledges "student learning and development" as a central point for use in the criteria

Regional associations accredit entire institutions (Young and others, 1983). These associations are responsible for a specific geographical region, of which there are six throughout the United States. The associations are Middle States Association of Colleges and Schools, New England Association of Schools and Colleges, North Central Association of Colleges and Schools, Northwest Association of Schools and Colleges, Southern Association of Colleges and Schools, and Western Association of Schools and Colleges. Their purpose is to evaluate the quality of the institution as a whole. Normally they do not try to ascertain quality for individual academic programs within the institution; however, a significant weakness in an individual program can alter a regional accreditor's evaluation (Commission on Institutions of Higher Education, 1983). Regional accreditation is typically reviewed every ten years (Middle States Association of Colleges and Schools, Commission on Higher Education, 1997). Each regional association may give specific focus or character to its accreditation process. For example, the Commission for Senior Colleges and Universities of the Western Association of Schools and Colleges Accrediting seeks to foster a "culture of evidence" among its member institutions through the self-study process (Wolff and Astin, 1990). In such an environment, an institution is open to receiving critical comments on its performance and can use data to respond to such comments. Regional accreditation provides recognition to institutions that meet a minimum standard of quality. Institutions then must strive to maintain this level of quality while seeking to improve human, physical, and financial resources; programs and services; and impact on students and other constituents. In order to maintain accreditation, an institution must respond to any criticism or suggestions given and work to improve the problems identified. Through this process, regional accreditation provides opportunities for institutional improvement and accountability.

The regional accreditation process has three phases: institution self-study, external review, and final decision by the regional commission on accreditation (or reaccreditation). The first phase consists of a probe of the institution or specific programs for which accreditation is sought by a team drawn from within the institution under review (Young and others, 1983). Self-study is conducted through review guidelines established by the accrediting body conducting the review. The accrediting body uses the self-study to evaluate the strengths and weaknesses of the institution in the areas of goals, student composition, faculty qualifications, program structure and content, support services to students, and administrative services, which includes the physical plant, organization, governance, financial areas, research, public services, and outcomes (Young and others, 1983). The self-study aids in the improvement of institutions by helping to establish the foundation for planning, the expansion of research and self-analysis, a chance to review policies, increasing openness among the different factions of university, and helping staff to develop (Young and others, 1983). Accreditors assert that a well-developed and thorough self-study can give an institution a tool for planning and self-analysis (Middle States Association of Colleges and Schools, Commission on Higher Education, 1997). The first phase of self-study can provide valuable information that can serve to promote change.

The next phase brings the accrediting body, chosen by the accrediting association, to campus to conduct an on-site review. The team members are typically from the academic community of similar institutions who serve as peers of the institution under review. They can include various stakeholders and quality assurance agencies (Ewell, 1998). The team's final report is based on the review of the self-study presented by the institution, additional evidence gathered during their site visit, and their professional opinions. A constructive exit interview with institutional leadership and the self-study team allows the reviewers to provide appropriate advice to institutions on how they may improve their quality. The reviewers also make a recommendation to the association based on their findings. The external reviewers serve as a liaison between the institution and the accrediting body.

In the third phase, a committee of the accrediting association, whose members are most often professionals and faculty in the field, reviews the final report submitted by the external review team. It then makes a decision about whether accreditation (or reaccreditation) should be granted. The committee suggests specific areas in which the institution can improve its effectiveness and may pose a variety of institutional courses of action depending on the context and the issue addressed. The final decision made in this third phase completes the accreditation process.

Regional accreditation is a process intended to improve the quality of institutions. Society holds higher education accountable for providing evidence that students are receiving the maximum yield possible from their personal, financial, academic, and emotional investment. Higher education institutions are considered "vendors" in an economy in which the perspective of the consumer is central (Braskamp and Braskamp, 1997). Society demands "product guarantees," and accreditation provides the stamp of approval (Uehling, 1987). To receive this approval, institutions are subject to the three phases in the regional accreditation process. All phases demand adherence to quality and integrity (Uehling, 1987). They serve to identify potential problems within an institution or program and provide a statement of quality to external stakeholders.

Initiatives in Accreditation

The nature of accreditation as a voluntary process has changed over the years. A review of the recent evolution of regional accreditation reveals a transition from an initially voluntary nature to one that is increasingly mandatory.

Voluntary accreditation is a complex story of American institutions' seeking to maintain quality and integrity in education. When institutional eligibility for receipt of federal funding was attached to regional accreditation, the voluntary nature of such accreditation became largely involuntary. Today regional accreditation remains a nongovernmental pursuit, but tension remains between the federal government and higher education, particularly following the failed introduction of State Postsecondary Review Entities in 1965. Colleges and universities and their constituent associations have joined to form several voluntary agencies to coordinate regional and programmatic accreditation. Since 1995, the most recent of these, the CHEA has sought to restore the voluntary nature of the accreditation process to its original purpose: promoting quality. Along with CHEA, regional accrediting bodies have started initiatives aimed at creating a national agenda.

The U.S. Department of Education proposed changes in June 1999 to the 1998 Higher Education Act that directly affected accrediting agencies. Among the several key issues, agencies are expected to review distance-education programs using the same standards they use for evaluating other academic programs (Healy, 1999). If an institution were developing off-campus locations, the accreditors would be required to visit only the first three locations, after which they could use their own discretion. The U.S. secretary of education would take on a new role of setting deadlines for the improvement of accrediting agencies that are experiencing problems. "Unannounced campus visits" were no longer expected as part of the review process. Accreditors would be required to do a periodic review of their own standards to comply with issues of reliability and validity better. All of these changes are in the spirit of making the process of accreditation more flexible and, to some extent, more collegial. For example, the Middles States Association is currently concluding such a review. The proposed regulations seek to return to the traditional role of accreditation: assessing quality and helping institutions become better places of learning (Healy, 1999).

In order for institutions to become better places of learning, each of the regional accrediting associations has undertaken a variety of projects and activities. Under the aegis of the CHEA, the six regional accrediting bodies have sought to foster similar goals and practices. Each has identified its purpose and defined initiatives that serve to improve the process of regional accreditation, as well as improve the connection between regional accreditation and student outcomes assessment. These initiatives range from surveys concerning accreditation standards to new frameworks dealing with outcomes assessment. Each of the initiatives is unique, but its underpinnings adhere to similar ideals of Continuous Quality Improvement (CQI) and collegiality among institutions and their accrediting bodies.

Current Initiatives of the Regional Accrediting Bodies

In July 1999, the North Central Association of Colleges and Schools (NCACS) embarked on the development of a new framework for accreditation. Its Academic Quality Improvement Project is based on helping higher-education institutions develop individual efforts at promoting systematic and continuous improvement. This new model maintains a focus on educational quality while preserving the ideas of institutional autonomy and distinctiveness. The project emphasizes the connection between assessment and accreditation standards. The NCACS is also involved in a project revising its mission and purpose.

The New England Association of Schools and Colleges (NEASC) conducted a survey of chief executive officers in 1998–1999 that sought to determine if the standards for accreditation were capable of assessing the effectiveness of their individual institutions. This initiative is aimed at involving institutions further in the standards that assess their educational quality. The NEASC has conducted an additional survey to learn more about its members' procedures for increasing institutional effectiveness through student outcomes assessment.

The Western Association of Schools and Colleges (WASC) has organized current initiatives around the word *dialogue,* defined as communication among institutions. Since 1997, WASC has recognized and promoted the importance of sharing and communicating best practices in assessing student learning outcomes and other areas of significance with institutions and other regional accrediting bodies. WASC also revised its standards along three dimensions: reducing the number of standards to simplify the regional accreditation process, shifting the stance of accreditation from compliance to collaboration, and giving emphasis to educational effectiveness and student learning.

The other regional accrediting bodies—the Commission on Colleges of the Southern Association of Colleges and Schools (SACS), the Northwest Association of Schools and Colleges (NASC), and the Commission on Higher Education of the Middle States Association of Schools and Colleges

(MSASC)—also have stimulated initiatives aimed at enhancing educational quality, promoting greater collaboration among accrediting bodies and institutions, and emphasizing the assessment of student learning outcomes. SACS modified their criteria to allow members confident of meeting basic SACS standards to augment the self-study process with "strategic visits," which give external input and counsel to the institution on its chosen directions for future development of the institution. Institutions need to demonstrate educational quality continually in addition to doing so when they are granted accreditation. SACS is demonstrating the viability of continual visits to improve the process of accreditation, the institution's self-study, and the ability to transfer standards of quality to working examples of change.

In 1996, the MSA issued Framework for Outcomes Assessment, which emphasized that the goal of outcomes assessment is improvement of teaching and learning. The framework supports the idea that student outcomes assessment should attempt to determine the extent and quality of the learning students are receiving. This can be done through the nine steps in the framework assessment plan, which MSA has provided to its members. MSA also is concluding a review of its standards to sharpen the standards relative to the teaching and learning processes of institutions.

As we shall see in subsequent chapters, the six regional accrediting bodies, by adhering to a national agenda focused on improving the regional accreditation process, have created changes and programs and started initiatives that also affect the other regional accrediting bodies, specialized accrediting bodies, and institutions of higher education. These initiatives, along with a close adherence to collaboration among entities, will serve to improve the regional accreditation process by incorporating specific criteria relative to student outcomes assessment.

Student Outcomes Assessment

The shift toward more student-centered and learning-oriented accreditation standards that began in the mid-1980s links student outcomes assessment and accreditation.

In the mid-1980s, calls for reform in higher education were heeded by national reports. Reports such as *Involvement in Learning* (Study Group on the Conditions of Excellence in American Higher Education, 1984), *Integrity in the College Curriculum* (American Association of Colleges, 1985), and *Time for Results* (National Governors' Association, 1986) stimulated a conversation between government representatives about student learning outcomes and the preparation of college graduates (Banta and Moffett, 1987). Individual institutional pioneers in implementing student learning outcomes as a priority included Alverno College in Milwaukee, WI, Truman State University in Kirksville, MO, and the University of Tennessee, Knoxville (Banta, 1985; Palomba and Banta, 1999). Although these individual institutions implemented assessment programs in the 1980s, the majority of assessment programs began as a result of statewide initiatives. Since the early 1980s, states increasingly have mandated the documentation of student outcomes. Formal state-level interaction began with Tennessee and Virginia. In 1979, Tennessee adopted a policy that granted funding based on standardized testing and student outcome assessment results. A different model in Virginia emerged in 1985, where institutions choose their own assessment procedures to reflect individual institutional missions (National Center for Education Statistics, 1996). The institutional autonomy inherent in Virginia's model is a more accepted model of state-mandated student outcomes assessment. In 1984, Florida began a statewide student assessment program, the College Level Academic Skills Test. These examples portray very different state initiatives. In fact, no two states have identical policies regarding accreditation or assessment (Paulson, 1990). Nevertheless, since 1985, state mandates and regional accreditation criteria have required most colleges and universities to implement procedures for student outcomes assessment (Borden and Bottrill, 1994).

In the fall of 1988, William Bennett, the U.S. secretary of education, suggested that accreditation organizations incorporate criteria for institutional student outcomes into their accrediting criteria (U.S. Department of Education, 1988). Over the next few years, regional and programmatic accrediting bodies issued new guidelines for accreditation that included student outcomes assessment. The role of statewide initiatives was crucial to stimulating the kind of attention being paid to student outcomes. Today these initiatives are reinforced by the standards of the regional accreditation agencies (El-Khawas, 1993).

Rossman and El-Khawas (1987) suggest three reasons that assessment exists in higher education institutions: political, economic, and educational. Erwin (1991) proposes a fourth: societal. Political reasons include the need of government officials to ascertain that funds allocated to higher education are being used effectively for programs and services. Assessment is seen as a tool to ensure that colleges and universities produce graduates who constitute a well-trained, competent, and competitive workforce—the economic reason. Educational reasons for assessment often come from within higher education and are reflected in the various national reports. In these reports, quality is most often the primary educational reason for implementing assessment. The societal reason refers to the broader public aspect of higher education. Society needs to understand what higher education is offering and how it is meeting the needs of the public. Such social concerns extend beyond the immediate needs of government officials for attestation that public funds are being used wisely and are larger than the internal academic discourse over the quality of programs and services.

The reasons given for why assessment exists are closely related to why accreditation exists. Federal and state governments are interested in both assessment and regional accreditation because they have a vested interest in knowing how funding is spent. Given increasingly tight budget restrictions, the federal and state governments are forced to take a more active role in determining the outcomes and quality of institutions for the money invested. Economically, the issue is providing quality institutions that will produce quality learning to ensure a capable and proficient workforce. This translates into positive student outcomes, and these students become productive, contributing members to the economy. Educationally, the assessment of learning is important, and curricular reform may be necessary to produce a quality learning experience. Increasing tuition costs and parental concern provide reasons for the societal concerns relating to assessment (Erwin, 1991). The rationale for student outcomes assessment helps define its scope and the methods of implementation.

Assessing Student Learning Outcomes

Student learning outcomes are commonly defined as "any change or consequence occurring as a result of enrollment in a particular educational institution and involvement in its programs" (Ewell, 1983). Assessment is the process of defining, selecting, designing, collecting, analyzing, interpreting, and using information to increase students' learning and development (Marchese, 1987). A framework is often useful in organizing and coordinating the process. One such framework offers five dimensions (Rowntree, 1987).

The first dimension of Rowntree's framework addresses the question: Why assess? This involves deciding why assessment needs to be conducted and what can be expected as a result. There are many purposes of assessment. For example, assessment can be used in maintenance of standards, admissions, motivation of students, and feedback purposes for both teachers and students. The purposes of assessment may overlap and be reciprocal or can conflict. An example of where two purposes of assessment reciprocate can be found in selecting a group of candidates who score extremely high on standardized tests. An institution may be improving its standards because it will have a student body that entered at a higher level than in the past. An example where purposes may conflict is providing feedback to a student within the confines of a course. This may detrimentally affect that particular student's motivation. The above purposes of assessment do not exhaust possible reasons for conducting assessment. Other reasons for conducting assessment include demonstrating external accountability, recruiting, fundraising, and improving instruction (Ewell, 1998). It is very important that an institution or program decide on and state the purpose of assessment beyond that of fulfilling accreditation requirements. Most purposes of assessment revolve around improving performance in some aspect or demonstrating effectiveness. Both involve some aspect of evaluation that is making judgments about the efforts of assessment (Ratcliff, 1996). These two concepts are also related to the differentiation between formative and summative assessment.

The second dimension of Rowntree's framework focuses on the question: What to assess? Given the exploration of the variety of student outcomes, it is difficult to determine which are most important. Four types of outcomes emerge: cognitive-psychological, cognitive-behavioral, affective-psychological, and affective-behavioral (Astin, 1973). The variety of possible student outcomes makes the process of assessment difficult to implement. Given individual institutions, different populations of students, varying state regulations, and a variety of student learning taxonomies, what to assess has become an individual institutional decision based on mission and institutional goals.

The third dimension addresses the question: How to assess? This dimension entails selection of a way to describe student learning from the many possible choices. The methods and measures selected should describe and differentiate excellent, satisfactory, and unsatisfactory performance. The criteria and measures selected often imply a method of data collection as well as integrating assessments from out-of-class experiences and in-class experiences, which can yield better judgments about what a particular student is learning than relying on one measure (Ewell, 1983). Also, it may be useful to incorporate both traditional and nontraditional assessment measures, such as interviews, self-judgment of one's own learning, and practical skills tests.

The fourth dimension answers the question: How to interpret? After obtaining results from the selected measures, the next step is exploring the results. Understanding this aspect of the framework is extremely important for each person in the assessment process. Data do not render their own significance. A low undergraduate performance on a writing assessment may mean that the institution needs to give more attention to improving student abilities in that area. Or it may mean that the writing assessment chosen does not adequately reflect the type of writing skills taught. Or it may mean that students are not being asked to write and improve their writing in the first courses they select in college. The results of the writing assessment alone will not illuminate where the problem lies. Further inquiry is required for improvement to occur. This further inquiry provides the interpreters of the results with a yardstick by which to measure the outcomes in the future as well.

The fifth dimension considers the question: How to respond? This involves determining to whom to communicate the findings and through what medium. Rowntree (1987) presumes two important things to consider in how to respond: providing the information to the public and providing information that is accurate and detailed. The greater the amount of information that an institution can provide, the more valid and reliable the assessment procedure will be. Also, by using honest information, the institution can consider its assessment process a means to change and improve its practices.

This framework provides only a beginning. It allows programs and institutions to organize their thoughts and give a sense of direction to a complicated process. It is also useful to determine what goes into assessing. Banta, Lund, Black, and Oblander (1996) stated: "A general theme running throughout appeals for reform is the need for institutions to focus their assessment efforts on what matters most" (p. 4). Institutions can use this framework as a way to determine where and how assessment efforts would matter most based on mission, goals, outcomes, and expectations.

Putting Accreditation and Assessment Together: Some Conclusions

Assessment and accreditation are both premised on the importance of quality assurance. Everyone in the educational enterprise has responsibility for maintaining and improving the quality of services and programs. Equally important are regular reviews of the validity and viability of the systems for examining quality. Colleges and universities, which seriously value and undertake quality assurances (including peer reviews), normally engage in a self-critical and reflective process. This process includes all members of the community as they strive to contribute to and enhance the educational enterprise.

The formal self-study and review process relies on certain key attributes in order to formulate strong plans. First, it should be "clear to all parties concerned (government, parliament, higher education institutions—staff and students) what may be expected from such a review process (Vroeijenstijn, 1995, p. 39). Clear expectations defining the purposes and the outcomes to be achieved through review processes must be articulated and shared with all participants. Major purposes of evaluating quality can include contributing to decisions on planning or funding, validating, granting professional recognition to programs, accrediting, or making awards of degrees (Frazer, 1991). Reviews also need to define whether the focus is on teaching, student learning, or research.

Second, the review process should be directed toward either a summative or formative evaluation. Attempts to conduct both simultaneously may lead to less successful efforts. Formative evaluations are most useful in providing directions for programmatic improvements, which faculty and administrators most highly value.

Third, college and universities should have direct responsibility and active engagement in the review processes. Taking self-study and student assessments seriously as means to accountability and improvement helps faculty and administrators to gain commitment and ownership for both the process and the outcomes. The results are more likely to be viewed as useful and credible by faculty and will have more potential to lead to targeted enhancements. Fourth, these review processes are not ends in themselves but represent ongoing processes that should be constantly refined or adapted to changing conditions within and external to the institutional environment. Regular, systematic, and cyclical reviews help institutions to monitor the strengths of their system continuously, with a particular focus on the types of improvements made after each evaluation cycle.

There is a growing consensus that effective quality assurance methods such as accreditation and program review will depend on the history, traditions, and culture of the country, state, or territory concerned. Whatever these may be for a particular program or institution, an external element to the processes selected is necessary to attain a clear, objective, and credible outcome (Bethel, 1991). Increasingly, faculty and administrators value the views emanating from peer evaluations in crafting the course of reform.

Most countries recognize that the need to sustain or develop their economies requires an increasing population of skilled individuals to achieve stability and meet competitive challenges in the world. Escalating costs of higher education and increased student access have led to significant growth and complexity in U.S. colleges and universities. External constituencies, including employers and the public, will continue to want evidence that higher education is meeting the needs of the workplace and society in general.

The formal review processes discussed here outline the important roles that accreditation and program review have in aiding institutions to improve and inform their constituents. University alumni will assume expanded roles as citizens who must address complex issues in society and will assume leadership positions in industry and commerce. Also, sustaining basic and applied research is necessary if the skills needed by society and the global economy are to be reached.

The introduction of student outcomes assessment in the early 1980s with Tennessee and Virginia demonstrated a movement in higher education largely characterized by increased state intervention. Statewide mandates often brought about the need for student outcomes assessment plans. From the early 1980s through 1988, states increasingly became involved in mandating student outcomes assessment, and institutions felt an infringement on institutional autonomy. Beginning with the urgings of U.S. Secretary of Education William Bennett in 1988, accrediting bodies began to incorporate student outcomes assessment into the accreditation criteria.

The accountability movement in the 1990s followed the campus-based assessment movement of the 1980s (Gaither, 1995). Accountability put accreditation and assessment on a collision course. Two parallel continuums can be seen: one detailing the cycle of accreditation and the other student outcomes assessment. Now the two continuums have merged. The accountability movement is still an active issue in higher education. The chapters that follow illustrate how these can be positive forces in public accountability, the impetus for internal change, the extension of distance learning, and accreditation processes.

References

American Association of Colleges. *Integrity in the College Curriculum: A Report to the Academic Community.* Washington, D.C.: American Association of Colleges, 1985.

Astin, A. "Measurement and Determinants of the Outputs of Higher Education. In L. Solmon and P. Taubman, P. (eds.), *Does College Matter? Some Evidence on the Impacts of Higher Education.* Orlando, Fla.: Academic Press, 1973.

Banta, T. W. "Use of Outcomes Information at the University of Tennessee, Knoxville." In P. T. Ewell (ed.), *Assessing Educational Outcomes.* New Directions for Institutional Research, no. 47. San Francisco: Jossey-Bass, 1985.

Banta, T. W., Lund, J. P., Black, K. E., and Oblander, F. W. *Assessment in Practice: Putting Principles to Work on College Campuses.* San Francisco: Jossey-Bass, 1996.

Banta, T. W., and Moffett, M. S. "Performance Funding in Tennessee: Stimulus for Program Improvement." In D. F. Halpern, *Student Outcomes Assessment: What Institutions Stand to Gain.* New Directions for Higher Education, no. 59. San Francisco: Jossey-Bass, 1987

Barak, R. J. *Program Review in Higher Education: Within and Without.* Boulder, Colo.: National Center on Higher Education Management Systems. ERIC Document Reproduction No. ED 246 829, 1982.

Bethel, D. "Conclusions." In Craft, A. (ed.), *Quality Assurance in Higher Education: Proceedings of an International Conference Hong Kong.* Washington, D. C.: The Falmer Press, 1991.

Borden, V.M.H., and Bottrill, K. V. "Performance Indicators: History, Definitions, and Methods." In V.M.H. Borden and T. W. Banta (eds.), *Using Performance Indicators to Guide Strategic Decision Making.* New Directions for Institutional Research, no. 82. San Francisco: Jossey-Bass, 1994.

Braskamp, L. A., and Braskamp, D. C. "The Pendulum Swing of Standards and Evidence." *CHEA Chronicle,* July 1997, p. 5. [http://www.chea.org/Chronicle/vol1/no5/index.html].

Commission on Institutions of Higher Education, New England Association of Schools and Colleges. *Accreditation Handbook: 1983 Edition.* Winchester, Mass.: New England Association of Schools and Colleges, 1983.

Council for Higher Education Accreditation. "Why CHEA?" *CHEA Chronicle,* Nov. 1996, 1(3). [http://www.chea.org/Chronicle/vol1/no3/index.html].

Eggers, W. "The Value of Accreditation in Planning." *CHEA Chronicle,* Jan. 2000, (3)1. [http://www.chea.org/Chronicle/vol3/no1/value.html].

El-Khawas, E. *Higher Education Panel Report No. 83.* Washington, D.C.: American Council on Education, 1993.

Erwin, T. D. *Assessing Student Learning and Development: A Guide to the Principles, Goals, and Methods of Determining College Outcomes.* San Francisco: Jossey-Bass, 1991.

Ewell, P. T. *Information on Student Outcomes: How to Get It and How to Use It.* Boulder, Colo.: National Center for Higher Education Management Systems, 1983.

Ewell, P. T. *Assessment, Accountability and Improvement.* Washington, D.C.: American Association for Higher Education, 1987.

Ewell, P. T. *Examining a Brave New World: How Accreditation Might Be Different.* Boulder, Colo.: National Center for Higher Education Management Systems, 1998.

Frazer, M. "Quality Assurance in Higher Education." In Craft, A. (ed.), *Quality Assurance in Higher Education: Proceedings of an International Conference Hong Kong.* Washington, D.C.: The Falmer Press, 1991.

Gaither, G. H. (ed.) *Assessing Performance in an Age of Accountability: Case Studies.* New Directions for Higher Education, no. 91. San Francisco: Jossey-Bass, 1995.

George, M. D. "Assessing Program Quality." In Wilson, R. F. (ed.), *Designing Academic Program Reviews.* New Directions for Higher Education, no. 37. San Francisco: Jossey-Bass, 1982.

Halpern, D. F. "Student Outcomes Assessment: Introduction and Overview." In D. F.

Halpern (ed.), *Student Outcomes Assessment: What Institutions Stand to Gain.* New Directions for Higher Education, no. 59. San Francisco: Jossey-Bass, 1987.

Healy, P. "Education Department Proposes Rules to Increase Flexibility In Accreditation." *Chronicle of Higher Education,* July 9, 1999.

Kells, H. R. *Self-Regulation in Higher Education: A Multi-National Perspective on Collaborative Systems of Quality Assurance and Control.* Higher Education Policy Series, no. 15. London: Jessica Kingsley Publishers, 1992.

Marchese, T. "Third Down, Ten Years to Go." *AAHE Bulletin,* 1987, *40,* 3–8.

McGuinness, A. C. "The States and Higher Education." In P. G. Altbach, R. O. Berdahl, and P. J. Gumport (eds.), *American Higher Education in the Twenty-First Century: Social, Political, and Economic Challenges.* Baltimore, Md.: Johns Hopkins University Press, 1999.

Middle States Association of Colleges and Schools, Commission on Higher Education. *Directory: Accredited Membership and Candidates for Accreditation, 1997-98.* Philadelphia: Commission on Higher Education, 1997.

National Center for Education Statistics. *The National Assessment of College Student Learning: State-Level Assessment Activities, a Report of the Proceedings of the Third Study Design Workshop.* Washington, D.C.: National Center for Education Statistics, 1996.

National Governors' Association. *Time for Results: The Governor's 1991 Report on Education.* Washington, D.C.: National Governors' Association Center for Policy Research and Analysis, 1986.

Palomba, C. A., and Banta, T. W. *Assessment Essentials: Planning, Implementing, and Improving Assessment in Higher Education.* San Francisco: Jossey-Bass, 1999.

Paulson, C. P. *State Initiatives in Assessment and Outcome Measurement: Tools for Teaching and Learning in the 1990s: Individual State Profiles.* Denver: Education Commission of the States, 1990.

Ratcliff, J. L. "Assessment, Accreditation, and Evaluation of Higher Education in the US." *Quality in Higher Education,* 1996, 2(1).

Ratcliff, J. L. "Institutional Self-Evaluation and Quality Assurance: A Global View." In A. Strydom and L. Lategan (eds.), *Enhancing Institutional Self-Evaluation in South African Higher Education: National and International Perspectives.* Blomfontein, RSA: Unit for Research in Higher Education, University of the Orange Free State, 1998.

Rossman, J. E., and El-Khawas, E. *Thinking About Assessment: Perspectives for Presidents and Chief Academic Officers.* Washington, D.C.: American Council on Education and American Association for Higher Education, 1987.

Rowntree, D. *Assessing Students: How Shall We Know Them?* New York: Nichols Publishing Company, 1987.

Study Group on the Conditions of Excellence in American Higher Education, National Institute of Education. *Involvement in Learning: Realizing the Potential of American Higher Education.* Washington, D.C.: U.S. Government Printing Office, 1984.

Uehling, B. S. "Serving Too Many Masters: Changing the Accreditation Process." *Educational Record,* 1987, *68*(3), 38–41.

U.S. Department of Education. "Secretary's Procedures and Criteria for Recognition of Accrediting Agencies." *Federal Register,* 1988, *53*(127), 25088–25099.

van Vught, F. A. "Intrinsic and Extrinsic Aspects of Quality Assessment in Higher Education." In Westerheijden, D. F., Brennan, J., and Massen, P. A. M. (eds.), *Changing Contexts of Quality Assessment.* Utrecht: Lemma, 1994.

van Vught, F. A., and Westerheijden, D. F. *Quality Management and Quality Assurance in European Higher Education: Methods and Mechanisms.* Luxembourg: Office for Office Publications, European Community, 1993.

Vroeijenstijn, A. I. *Improvement and Accountability: Navigating Between Scylla and Charybdis: Guide for External Quality Assessment in Higher Education.* Higher Education Policy Series, no. 30. Bristol, Pa.: Jessica Kingsley Publishers, 1995.

Wolff, R. A., and Astin, A. W. "Assessment 1990: Accreditation and Renewal." Paper presented at the Fifth American Association of Higher Education Conference on Assessment in Higher Education, Washington, D.C., 1990.

Young, K. E., and others. *Understanding Accreditation*. San Francisco: Jossey-Bass, 1983.

EDWARD S. LUBINESCU is a doctoral candidate and graduate research assistant at the Shreyer Institute for Teaching and Learning, Pennsylvania State University.

JAMES L. RATCLIFF is president of Performance Associates Postsecondary Consulting in Pueblo, Colorado and is affiliate senior scientist and former director of the Center for the Study of Higher Education at Pennsylvania State University.

MAUREEN A. GAFFNEY is a doctoral candidate and graduate research assistant in higher education at Pennsylvania State University.

2

This chapter examines what types of student learning outcomes are amendable to assessment for the purposes of accreditation.

The Student Learning Self-Study: Choices and Opportunities

Susan R. Hatfield

Like legislators, state higher education executive offices, the general public, and students themselves, regional and professional accrediting agencies have taken a keen interest in student learning. It is no longer enough for universities and departments to assert that the educational process has resulted in student learning. Instead, accrediting agencies are asking for documentation that supports the assertion that students have indeed achieved the desired learning goals and, just as important, an indication of the steps to be taken to close any gaps between departmental goals and student performance. While universitywide efforts might be useful in assessing the overall success of the institution in achieving its goals, student learning must be assessed at the department or program level.

Making Choices about Assessing Learning

Departments and programs undertaking an accreditation self-study focusing on student learning must (1) define the learning goals for their students, (2) identify how those outcomes are facilitated through the curriculum and structured learning experiences, and (3) design and implement assessment processes and methods. The department or program must have identified specific learning goals for their students, promoted those goals through a set of specifically designed learning activities, and made conscious decisions as to how those goals can be best measured.

Setting Goals. In her study of 440 reports gathered between 1993 and 1995, Lopez (1996) from the North Central Association of Colleges and

NEW DIRECTIONS FOR HIGHER EDUCATION, no. 113, Spring 2001 © Jossey-Bass, A Publishing Unit of John Wiley & Sons, Inc.

Schools (which accredits over nine hundred institutions of higher education) found that

> evaluators [who visit schools as part of the accreditation process] praise academic units' assessment plans and programs when the unit uses its own statement of purpose and educational objectives to frame its statements about the characteristics and competencies it intends its students to acquire in a given major or graduate program. They found it important for faculty to establish measurable learning objectives for what they expect their students to learn [p. 9].

Lopez (1996) noted that evaluators regularly recommend that every academic department determine the extent to which each objective actually contributes to the incremental learning of its students. While the college or university usually identifies the general goals for student learning (which are operationalized, at least in theory, through the general educational curriculum), the disciplinary learning goals must be set by those on the front line: faculty members responsible for teaching in the program or department.

There are numerous choices a department, program, or discipline needs to make to be prepared to assess student learning. The process of making appropriate assessment choices begins with the understanding of departmental assessment as a continuous improvement cycle:

• Resources—what flows into the department
• Processes—what is being done to facilitate student learning
• Results—the student outcomes
• Feedback—how the results transform resources and processes

Historically, university-level assessment has been input or resource based, evaluating the effectiveness of an institution based on the scores of incoming students on national standardized tests and the size of the institution's endowment. Since most departments and programs do not directly control the resources available for their department (for instance, department budgets are determined by the administration), holding themselves accountable for the resources allocated to them is not sound assessment practice at the departmental level. Adequate resources are certainly an important issue for departments, but unless college and university administrations demonstrate budgeting and staffing decisions based on department needs and not on formulas or historical precedent, resources should not be a basis for department-level assessment of student learning.

Departmental processes, on the other hand, such as the curriculum, advising, and teaching-learning experiences, are under the direct control of the department or program faculty and should be assessed since the student learning outcomes are related to the quality of learning experiences and academic support that students receive. Measuring processes provides a starting point from which to begin if expectations do not match performance.

Student outcomes such as learning, satisfaction, and student development are critical components of a departmental assessment plan, with the caution that student learning should be featured prominently in the accreditation self-study. Measuring student satisfaction by itself does not provide evidence of student learning, nor does evidence of student growth and development.

Finally, departments and programs should consider goals for the quality of feedback they wish to receive from alumni, parents, community members, and employers, all of which may translate into resources (alumni by creating internships for current students or donating to the department) and process revision (feedback from employers identifying new skills needed in the workplace).

Process, outcome, and feedback goals should be studied on a continuous basis, perhaps through a program review process, in order to promote the ongoing improvement of the department. Although primarily focused on the discussion of student learning outcomes, the accreditation self-study will also need to address how the data on student learning are being used in the transformation of departmental processes or to build the case for additional resources, as well as include a reflective self-analysis of the department's assessment plan and implementation.

The continuous improvement cycle should begin with clear departmental goals that identify what a student can expect to gain as a result of studying a particular field or discipline. For example, these outcome goals may include student learning, student development, and student satisfaction. More specifically, student learning outcomes cluster in three areas: cognitive outcomes (what students should know), behavioral outcomes (what students should be able to do), and affective outcomes (attitudinal development). Cognitive outcomes might include the knowledge of a certain set of historical facts, key theories, essential processes, or the accepted set of criteria used by professionals in the field to evaluate a piece of evidence (see the taxonomy of cognitive objectives in Bloom, 1956). Behavioral outcomes are skill based, involving the demonstrated ability to perform a specific skill with an identified level of success. Affective outcomes "are directed toward a person, object, place, or idea and predispose individuals to behave in certain ways" (Palomba and Banta, 1999, p. 29). Like cognitive and behavioral outcomes, affective outcomes are developmental, demonstrating the student's growth as a thinker in the discipline.

Department-level assessment plans should identify student learning goals in each of these domains. Departments need to identify specifically what they want their students to be able to know, do, feel, think, and believe as a result of study in a particular discipline. The discussions leading to the identification of goals are the most valuable dialogue in which a department can engage and should not be undertaken lightly. In many cases, these discussions have never happened, as department members inherited a curriculum representing ghosts of faculties past, which may have been based more on what individuals wanted to teach (so-called pet rock courses) than on creating a coherent curriculum leading to specific, demonstrable learning outcomes.

While the emphasis of the accreditation self-study is on evaluating the results described, it is vital that departments broaden the treatment of assessment in their self-study and in practice to encompass issues of how the results are achieved (processes in place), what signs will signify whether the goals have been realized, and how performance gaps have been remedied. Results alone will not facilitate continuous improvement in a department because outcomes data alone do not offer clues as to what promoted the successful result or what may have contributed to students' lack of success. As such, related resources (financial, human, physical), relevant processes (such as curriculum, teaching, advising), and feedback (from employers, alumni, and internship supervisors) may help explain successes and failures.

Departments should engage issues concerning key department-level outcomes for their students, how those outcomes are facilitated, and the signs that the outcomes have been achieved. Without such knowledge, it is impossible to separate out random events from planned results.

Facilitating Outcomes: Random Effects versus Planned Results. Once the goals are created, departments and programs need to identify the characteristics of the academic program that facilitate achievement of the defined goals. If there is no plan for helping students achieve the desired goals, any success can as reasonably be attributed to a random effect as to a systematic program of study. It is at this point in the self-study processes that many departments and programs realize that although they may agree on the goals, they have no real coordinated effort in place to help students achieve success. At best, achievement is dependent on a student's progress through the curriculum in a certain sequence with specific instructors. Preparing the self-study may reveal that some of the key concepts (cognitive outcomes) or skill sets (behavioral outcomes) that have been identified as core knowledge in the discipline have always been assumed to have been part of the curriculum—yet those concepts and skills are never developed or emphasized in any course work. It also may become apparent that students have qualitatively different learning experiences depending on the instructor and elective path that they take through the curriculum. Until some coordination exists (and the ensuing discussion of academic freedom is resolved), departments cannot assume that students will learn the same thing from taking the same courses. The self-study process, coupled with data on student outcomes, permits the examination of how courses contribute, individually and collectively, to attaining program goals. As Stark and Lowther (1986) point out, there are a number of different curricula that exist: the one in the catalogue, the one the faculty are teaching, and the one that students are taking. For students to achieve a set of cognitive, behavioral, and affective outcomes, these curricula need to be coordinated in such a way that outcomes can be tied to the curriculum and not left up to chance.

Assessing the Outcomes. Methodologies for assessing student learning outcomes are dependent on the domain of the learning goals being assessed. For instance, assessing a skill or ability (public speaking, for instance) through a standardized multiple-choice test makes as little sense as measuring knowledge about a theory or concept through a student survey.

Cognitive outcomes involve the learning of the knowledge of the discipline, including the key theories, concepts, and applications. Common methodologies used in assessing the cognitive domain include pretest–posttest (where the net learning gain can be quantified), as well as capstone experiences, exams, projects, and oral exams (Lopez, 1996). As Lopez (1996) points out, scores on admission tests, progress in a master's program, successful completion of a course, and curriculum revisions do not constitute measures of student learning in this domain.

Behavioral learning outcomes involve the ability to demonstrate a specific set of identified skills or abilities, usually within a specific domain-related context. Common methodologies used to assess learning in the behavioral domain include juried recitals in the performing arts, presentations, demonstrations, longitudinal designs, and surveys of employers who have hired graduates (Lopez, 1996).

Affective learning outcomes involve the development of students' attitudes, beliefs, and values. According to Palomba and Banta (1999), examples of intended outcomes for the affective dimension include "being sensitive to the values of others, becoming aware of one's own talents and abilities, and developing an appreciation for lifelong learning. Practicing ethical behavior, exhibiting personal discipline, and providing leadership are other examples of intended outcomes that address attitudes and values" (p. 29).

The most common methodology for assessing learning in this domain is the use of self-report surveys, specifically those that employ a pretest-posttest design (Lopez, 1996), as well as focus groups. More objective data on learning in this domain can be obtained through observing group work and simulations and monitoring participation rates (Palomba and Banta, 1999).

Associating learning outcome domains with appropriate assessment methodologies is the first step in designing a department or program-level assessment plan. Implementing the plan requires additional considerations, such as whether to conduct formative or summative assessment, use quantitative or qualitative methodologies, and measure the goals individually or holistically.

Formative and Summative Assessment. Student learning can be assessed both formatively and summatively. Formative assessment takes place while the learning is in progress, providing an estimation of whether students are on track toward achieving the stated learning goals. This type of assessment can focus on individual students (which becomes very close to a student evaluation process) or cohorts of students. In either case, formative assessment can shorten the correction cycle by capturing issues prior to a student's graduation. For instance, if a student has not demonstrated adequate writing competency in a sophomore writing experience (noted as the result of a formative assessment activity), that student may be required to take an additional writing class or perhaps visit the campus writing center. If a number of students exhibit the same deficiencies, the department may need to reevaluate its writing requirement and perhaps add writing experiences to the required curriculum. This formative assessment activity (monitoring the writing skills of sophomores) will help both the students and the department. Students whose performance is identified as poor while still on campus will have the opportunity to improve their skills before they get into the workplace; the department benefits by knowing in advance that their graduating majors are writing at a desired level of competence.

Summative assessment occurs at the end of the learning process; it assesses the degree to which students have achieved the stated learning goals. Unlike formative assessment, which can be similar to a student evaluation process, pure summative assessment is cohort driven. Summative assessment examines the learning artifacts of a specific group of students (for instance, graduating majors in a specific program) at an ending point (the completion of a course sequence or on graduation) in an effort to understand the degree to which that group of students has achieved the learning goals defined by the discipline using a set of performance standards, key indicators, or rubrics. The efficacy of this type of assessment is found in how the assessment data are used to refine teaching methods, advising, and the curriculum.

Formative and summative assessment methodologies provide the department or program with evidence of their students' learning. The choice to use either or both types of assessment methodologies should be considered carefully. Because the accreditation self-study team is interested not only in data but how the data are used for improvement, formative assessment methodologies should be used only if the department is absolutely committed to remedial tracks for students who do not meet the established performance criteria at each measurement interval. Reporting that 45 percent of sophomores were not writing at the desired level on the departmental writing exam will draw negative feedback from the accreditation team if such data are not accompanied by an explanation of what the department did to help those students get their writing up to par prior to graduation. Nor can summative assessment results stand alone. They too must be accompanied by plans for process-level improvements in areas where students were found to be weak.

Quantitative and Qualitative Methodologies. Learning outcomes can be measured both quantitatively and qualitatively, and the self-study should contain both types of measurement. Quantitative data make it easy to create a baseline, compare cohorts of students over time, and identify statistical outliers; qualitative data provide a rich contextual dimension. Regardless of whether a department starts with quantitative or qualitative data, one provides a means of explaining and validating the other. Individual interviews might identify issues that should be included in a large-scale survey. Survey data may often provide a sense of the issues that can be better understood through focus group discussions. Self-studies that triangulate the methodologies in order to achieve a better understanding of the issue being assessed provide powerful evidence of the department or program's understanding of assessment and add credibility to the results obtained. The accreditation self-study should provide a combination of both types of data in an attempt to understand thoroughly the nature of the results and as a prerequisite for making changes in the department. Qualitative data might hint at a problem area; quantitative data might provide a sense of the size of the issue. Quantitative data might suggest an emerging issue for which qualitative data might help focus.

Individual and Holistic Outcomes. Finally, learning outcomes can be measured individually or holistically. It is possible to measure student learning on each separate learning goal using individual course assignments sprinkled throughout the curriculum or to take a holistic approach, which allows for the students' strengths to balance out weaknesses.

The measure of the outcomes individually is usually done through the assessment of a specific assignment late in the student's curriculum using a rubric, primary trait analysis, or a standardized exam or specific experience designed to assess a particular set of knowledge or skills. This should be made an assessment process, not a student evaluation process. If the assessment is based on a classroom assignment, it should be scored separately from the grading process of the course in which the artifact was created. This should be done so that an individual faculty member is not entirely responsible for the assessment of a learning outcome, and so that the artifact is viewed completely separately from the students' performance on other assignments in the course.

This type of assessment can measure learning in any of the domains, though the domains are usually assessed separately. There is one major disadvantage to using course-based individual learning outcome assessment: there is no guarantee that students who perform at an acceptable level during a specific class will be able to demonstrate the same acceptable level of knowledge or skill the following semester or after graduation.

Students (many of whom view their education as a seat-time requirement) in curricula that are sequenced topically (flat curriculum structures with few prerequisites) as opposed to sequentially (tall curriculum structures where the theory and skill bases build on earlier courses) tend to engage in "brain dumping" following the end of the semester as part of a "took the course, got the credit" attitude toward their education. Course-based learning outcome measurement is problematic in this scenario. Still, in universities with large numbers of transfer students and older-than-average students, course-based learning outcome assessment may make the most sense, since students may take years to complete the curriculum sequence and may have attended numerous universities in the process.

Holistic assessment methods blend the cognitive, behavioral, and affective domains, allowing for the assessment of the entire learning experience. Common holistic assessment methodologies are capstone experiences, projects, exams (oral or written), and portfolios, all of which can be assessed using a rubric and team of faculty assessors.

Truman State University, in Kirksville, MO, and Alverno College, in Milwaukee, WI, have highly developed university-level portfolio assessment methodologies, but many academic departments with professional accreditation (engineering, teacher education, nursing, and social work, to name a few) and others in liberal studies and fine and performing arts at colleges and universities across the country have solid holistic assessment programs in place.

As with qualitative and quantitative data, individual and holistic assessment of student learning can be combined effectively. Student portfolios that contain samples of authentic student work (from course assignments throughout a student's career) allow the department or program to focus assessment on either the learning goals individually or the portfolio as a whole. While the assessment of the individual performance components may provide a sense of how the student has developed over the course of his or her education, a holistic assessment approach might provide an indication of how well-equipped graduates are to face their futures as professionals in their field.

Whether to engage in formative or summative assessment, using qualitative or quantitative methodologies, that will be assessed either individually or holistically are all important decisions for a department or program to consider carefully. While the answers to these questions will be evidenced in the accreditation self-study, the learning outcome results reported would not be the only issue considered by the self-study team. The team, especially in the North Central accrediting region, will also be looking for evidence of the thinking that went into the assessment plan.

Assessing the Self-Study: A Possible Tool for Implementation

While the accreditation self-study should address student learning, the site team expects assessment to be evolving on campuses. Thus, in addition to assessing student learning, the self-study should provide an analysis of the culture of assessment within the department or program and across campus. Embedded in this analysis should be the identification of the strengths and weaknesses of the department's assessment initiatives and an outline of what steps are to be taken to move the assessment initiative forward.

The North Central Association of Colleges and Schools has recently developed the Levels of Implementation Matrix, which outlines four criteria against which universities, colleges, and departments can benchmark their progress (Lopez, 2000). By identifying characteristics in each of three levels of implementation (beginning stages, making progress, and maturing stages), the university and department can identify what additional steps or actions need to be taken to further their assessment initiatives. The criteria identified in the matrix are (1) Institutional Culture (mission and collective values), (2) Shared Responsibility (faculty, students), (3) Institutional Support (structures and resources), and (4) Efficacy of Assessment. Adapting these issues to the department level yields the following key questions for the self-study:

1. Departmental Culture
   A. Collective/Shared Values
      To what degree does the department demonstrate a shared understanding of the purposes, advantages, and limitations of assessment?
   B. Mission
      To what degree do the departmental mission and educational goals state the value the department places on student learning?
2. Shared Responsibility
   A. Faculty
      To what degree is faculty taking responsibility for ensuring that direct and indirect measures of student learning are aligned with the program's educational goals and measurable objectives?
      To what degree is faculty knowledgeable about assessment?
   B. Students
      To what degree are students familiar with the goals and purposes of assessment in general and the departmental goals specifically?
3. Departmental Support
   A. Resources
      To what degree is participation in assessment valued by the department in terms of release time, compensation, or acknowledgment of the scholarship of assessment?
      Is there a line item in the budget for departmental assessment activities?
   B. Structures
      Is there a departmental assessment committee?
      Is assessment part of the department's faculty development program?
4. Efficacy of Assessment
   To what degree has assessment data been discussed by members of the department?
   To what degree has assessment data promoted change in the department?

A departmental accreditation self-study should not only address the assessment of student learning, but also provide a self-assessment of the department's progress on its assessment initiatives. The self-study team will expect that the department's assessment initiative is a work in progress; thus, the key self-study questions provide an important dimension to the self-study. Regardless of whether the department is just getting started in assessing learning outcomes or has an established assessment program, the department self-study should be able to present a clear self-assessment of its efforts: where it has been, where it is at, and, most important, where it is heading. Regardless of how the accreditation visit fits with the department's time line for implementation of their assessment plan—even if it is just getting started and has yet to collect any data—the accreditation self-study should provide evidence that the department understands what needs to be done in order to have a fully functioning assessment program—specifically that the departmental culture supports assessment, there is shared responsibility for it, departmental support exists in terms of resources and structures, and there is an understanding of how assessment data are to be used.

Conclusion

While a college's or university's general goals for student achievement can be measured at the university level, the accreditation self-study must address student academic achievement in the discipline. Therefore, departments and programs must contribute to the accreditation self-study by assessing their students' learning at the departmental level. No one else is better equipped to make the important decisions regarding goals and assessment methodology than those in the discipline.

Starting with the identification of learning goals in the cognitive, behavioral, and affective domains, departments and programs should carefully consider questions of formative and summative assessment, the advantages and disadvantages of quantitative and qualitative data, and whether it makes sense to assess learning goals individually or holistically. In addition, regardless of where the department is in its assessment efforts at the time of the accreditation self-study and subsequent visit, the self-study should demonstrate a clear understanding of the culture, responsibilities, resources, and data uses necessary to move its assessment initiative forward to the point where student learning can be clearly and accurately documented.

References

Bloom, B. S. (ed.). *Taxonomy of Educational Objectives: The Classification of Educational Goals. Handbook 1: Cognitive Domain.* White Plains, N.Y.: Longman, 1956.

Lopez, C. L. *Opportunities for Improvement: Advice from Consultant-Evaluators on Programs to Assess Student Learning.* Chicago: North Central Accreditation Commission on Institutions of Higher Education, Mar. 1996.

Lopez, C. L. *Making Progress on Assessment: Using the Level of Implementation to Improve Student Learning.* Paper presented at the Pacific Rim Conference on Higher Education Planning and Assessment. University of Hawaii Hilo, Consortium for Assessment and Planning Support, June 2000.

Palomba, C. A., and Banta, T. W. *Assessment Essentials: Planning, Implementing and Improving Assessment in Higher Education.* San Francisco: Jossey-Bass, 1999.

Stark, J. S., and Lowther, M. A. *Designing the Learning Plan: A Review of Research and Theory Related to College Curricula.* Ann Arbor: National Center for Research on Postsecondary Teaching and Learning, University of Michigan, 1986. (ED 287 439)

SUSAN R. HATFIELD is assessment coordinator at Winona State University.

3

Accrediting associations are examining the new realities created by distance education.

Distance Education and Accreditation

Watson Scott Swail, Eva Kampits

Skeptics argue that the nation's rich history of regional accreditation may be overwhelmed by the tsunami of technologically mediated instruction. However, the rapid development of distance education also may be seen as a rising tide that raises all ships, offering an unprecedented opportunity for new learning together with the development of appropriate assessment processes. This chapter focuses on a likely evolutionary path that identifies the accreditation resources and processes necessary to respond to change in educational delivery systems with an appropriate system of quality assurance. As one accreditor remarked, "This is a golden opportunity to reinvigorate a long history of regional accreditation, spurred by the shift in redefining Mr. Chips to 'chips' and education that is anytime and anywhere" (R. Mandeville, personal interview, Sept. 13, 2000). We conclude with a list of questions rather than answers to help guide future investigation and action in accreditation.

The Changing Landscape of Higher Education

Higher education has enjoyed the luxury of adhering to constancy in the academy's offerings and approaches—seemingly regardless of technological, economic, or political changes in society. Standards and practices associated with postsecondary study of the 1900s were purposefully similar to those of the 1800s. And while content changed with the advance of science and technology, the pedagogy of the university remained the same.

The advent of educational technologies has threatened to alter the practice of higher education before, but none with the scale and scope that distance learning possesses. More than a century ago, Thomas Edison predicted that the cinema would replace books, forecasting subsequent revelations of

New Directions for Higher Education, no. 113, Spring 2001 © Jossey-Bass, A Publishing Unit of John Wiley & Sons, Inc.

televisions and VCRs replacing teachers and traditional classrooms. While these technologies have triggered excitement in the classroom, such multimedia have not contributed convincingly to marked or demonstrable improvement in learning. The combination of programming ease, as found in LOGO (developed in the late 1960s), together with aggressive introduction of PCs for K–12 users, provided additional learning tools with few strategies to assess learning outcomes. Indeed, learning seemed most apparent where computers were *not* aligned in rows, facing an instructor (as in traditional classes), or where they were *not* segregated to areas named as labs, invoking scientific inaccessibility rather than engagement. Beginning in 1968, Seymour Papert of MIT's Artificial Intelligence Laboratory initiated school-college partnerships that are now found in diverse sites, such as MIT's Media Laboratory and charter schools in Los Angeles. These partnerships typically involve students and teachers in circular pods, accessible throughout the schoolday and in any class. Rennselaer Polytechnic Institute, in Troy, NY, through its computer-assisted studio labs in the sciences, also offers a nontraditional approach to teaching with technology as an aid. Such convivial formats combined with the accessibility of the World Wide Web triggered significant change in educational practice. New technologies have enabled educators at all levels to implement strategies that place the student as learner and teacher as coach, a concept familiar to those conversant with school reform efforts such as the Coalition of Essential Schools.[1] Educators must now grapple with the definition of who is the coach and with what role technology plays. Pedagogy in the new media requires serious and rapid involvement of those experienced in evaluation and assessment. Educators have little choice in addressing this challenge when faced with the stunning and rapid introduction of distance-learning opportunities.

Technology has become the lever of change for higher education for a number of reasons. It could be argued that this change is a culmination of a number of factors, including the move toward a global economy and the growing interest of students and families in postsecondary studies. But we offer the following reasons that it is happening now, to the degree it is happening:

• *The Internet opened communication to the public.* In the late 1960s, faculty and researchers enjoyed and created the backbone of distributed computing options with the formation of the Internet's precursor, the DARPAnet (supported by the U.S. Defense Department). Options for university faculty expanded in the 1970s with several events, including a plan for networked computing for the White House, applications for industry (such as airline reservations and supermarket scanner codes), and the development of personal computers. The growth in e-mail usage illustrates the point. In 1985, there were 300,000 e-mail users registered worldwide (Jones, 1977). By September 2000, the United States and Canada alone accounted for over 161 million on-line users (NUA, 2000). Today there are over 377 million on-line users worldwide, and the world market is expanding at incredible rates of 5 to 6 percent each month. This explosion in technological innovation and usage has had a significant impact on American higher education.

• *Institutions of higher education (IHEs) recognized that on-line technologies expand their market.* Colleges and universities, as well as corporations and proprietary postsecondary institutions, began to see how the Web would promote distance-education and distributed-learning opportunities. According to the U.S. Department of Education, the number of IHEs offering distance education has increased by one-third since 1994–1995. By the end of the twentieth century, 44 percent of IHEs offered distance courses (U.S. Department of Education, 1999). The number of enrollments reached 1.3 million credit courses, about half of them provided by two-year colleges. Thirty percent of all distance-education courses now use the Web (Green, 2000), and that figure will grow dramatically over the next few years. Essentially, the Web has begun to erase the traditional boundaries set up through legislation and other regulations. Now institutions have more freedom to look beyond their traditional geographic market. For those up to the challenge, the world is literally their new stage.

• *Distance education has challenged the concept of traditional higher education.* Until the late 1900s, higher education was the acknowledged primary provider of adult learning and degree programs. During the 1980s and 1990s, nontraditional players came into the game, including for-profit institutions and corporate universities. For-profit entities, such as the University of Phoenix and Devry, Inc., have since become major players in adult learning. Since its founding in 1976, the University of Phoenix has become America's largest for-profit IHE, serving over sixty thousand students each year at over seventy sites and through distance education. More recently, other noninstitutional entities, such as Blackboard.com and e-college.com, have expanded the pool of distance providers. These e-firms supply technical services to help traditional IHEs get on-line. Partnerships between traditional IHEs and for-profit ventures, such as Onlinelearning.net, operated by UCLA, and Fathom.com, now challenge traditional formulas for how, where, and when learning takes place.[2]

"A New Way of Learning for a New Kind of Student" is the self-declared tag for Harcourt Higher Education.[3] Licensed to operate in the state of Massachusetts, with a Student Service Center in Pennsylvania, Harcourt's catalogue claims, "No on-campus classes, no registration lines to stand in . . . just high-quality education delivered via the power of the Internet" (Harcourt Higher Education, 2000). Similar are a number of on-line colleges, such as Barnes & Noble.com, a fee-for-service organization that offers on-line learning for those seeking degrees or simply professional development. The corporate business market adds complexity to the list of organizations involved in education; it is a burgeoning force in adult education, expected to reach over $7 billion by 2002, a thirty-five-fold increase since 1997 (*Investor's Business Daily,* 2000).

Absent accountability, quality assurance, and evaluation, distance learning increasingly attracts educational providers attuned to marketability and profit. Distance education in its many forms is changing our perceptions about how we communicate and learn on both business and personal levels. Consumers are conscious of the power of e-commerce and e-learning, and the ideals associated with "learning anytime-anywhere" are not lost on the public at large.

In the eyes of some consumers, increased competition for students among new distance-education providers, colleges, and universities has resulted in significant blurring of the lines in terms of what higher education is and for whom it exists. Higher education continues to become more complex than ever before and is much more difficult to compartmentalize and describe than in the past (Marchese, 1998). Although we still analyze IHEs in terms of conventional Carnegie classifications, their usefulness in the light of these new forms of learning continues to fade.

An important fact to consider is that much of the on-line, asynchronous course and degree work is aimed at professional and graduate-level students. The University of Phoenix, for example, is explicitly targeted to professional audiences interested in upgrading their education. A recent Office of Educational Research and Improvement report found that corporate vendors have provided approximately 2.4 million information technology certifications to some 1.6 million individuals worldwide since 1997 (Adelman, 2000). While a majority of the growing number of completely on-line programs for higher education remain non–credit bearing, serving the professional development interests of a broad number of adults holding baccalaureate or other degrees, distance education also influences and challenges the capacity of traditional providers to educate. It also invites particular attention by the accrediting associations as they reflect on and describe their standards in the review of distance-education programs to ensure that they reflect quality, integrity, and effectiveness.

A Question of Quality and Control

This expansion of higher and adult distance education puts into question traditional mechanisms for ensuring educational quality.[4] As Martin, Manning, and Ramaley discuss in Chapter Seven, the institution is ultimately a learning organization. But what type of quality need exist in this brave new world of distance learning? Need we be assured that Psychology 101 offered in Des Moines, IA is comparable to that offered in Chico, CA, or Columbia, SC? Can we be sure that someone who receives a degree on-line is gaining the same knowledge and intellectual development as someone who experiences education on campus? Are we heading for a bifurcation in terms of educational quality between on-line and traditional systems? Or will we create the necessary checks and balances to ensure that quality is quality, regardless of how it is disseminated? Many colleges and universities have presented their distance-learning courses and programs as one and the same as their resident instruction. Yet the public may question the quality of distance-learning efforts, particularly those taught by part-time faculty and adjunct lecturers. Will accreditors assume they are pushed to seemingly looser standards, or will they come to give even more attention to standards (Wellman, 2000; Chronicle of Higher Education, 2000)? Do alternative accreditation processes hinder an accrediting association's reliance on the self-evaluation process as a guide to institutional improvement?[5]

These are difficult questions to answer. Nonetheless, the future perception of higher education demands that issues of quality be resolved to some degree. Arguments about the advantages and disadvantages of on-line education remain incomplete and generate questions regarding the quality of the various initiatives. For example, doubters may argue that distance education lacks a systemic way to control for quality in the expanding on-line market. Proponents quickly—and justifiably—may respond that traditional higher education has never instituted those types of checks and balances. Although we embark on a new century, we continue to be burdened with the reality that course quality varies greatly from state to state, institution to institution, and even class to class. How do we ensure quality for all learners at all levels?[6]

The Institute for Higher Education Policy, in association with the National Education Association and Blackboard.com, recently released a set of twenty-four benchmarks for distance education as an initial set of standards for providers (Institute for Higher Education Policy, 2000). Although these benchmarks provide some indicators of effective practice, they are only recommendations for quality practice and lack the compelling authority for their implementation.

The Western Association of Schools and Colleges and the North Central Association of Colleges and Schools have established alternative assessment guidelines for distance-education programs. These may constitute a pragmatic approach inasmuch as they are based on a parallel, "separate but equal" track for institutions already accredited by traditional standards.

Federal standards are likely to come into play in 2001. The National Advisory Committee on Institutional Quality and Integrity, which evaluates accrediting associations' compliance with the U.S. Department of Education standards, is reconsidering how the accreditation and recognition of distance learning should be addressed in amendments to the Higher Education Act of 1998. Accrediting associations need to consider the implications of the U.S. Education Department's deferring action on policy that would expand current recognition practices to include distance education or, conversely, to legislating separate standards for distance learning. Recent discussions on Capitol Hill suggest that legislators will require that some gateway agency be created to validate the quality of distance education by 2002. Accreditors will need to contribute to the development of distance providers at the same time they consider how current or evolving standards might address concerns about strengths and weaknesses in the delivery system.

Beginning in autumn 2001, Congress will examine whether the distance-learning industry has assumed responsibility for self-regulation and quality assurance. Legislators already have made it known that they would consider imposing regulations on the industry should they contemplate expanding public oversight of these programs (Ludes, 2000). Accreditors will need to be attentive to the shift that may take place should distance education be removed from the scope of activities of the recognized accrediting associations. Ultimately accreditors will need to address the challenges of distance education, regardless of the pace of previous attention.

With unforeseen alacrity, the regional associations have formed a transregional discussion and collaboration on what serves as an appropriate evaluation of distance education. The newly formed Council of Regional Accrediting Commissions will act on guidelines for site-based institutions involved in distance education in February 2001.[7] These further recommendations regarding best practices in electronically offered programming were initially drafted by the Western Cooperative for Educational Telecommunications with facilitation by the Council for Higher Education Accreditation (CHEA).[8]

Regional Accreditation Serving a National Constituency

In the past two decades, distance education has moved from an array of on-line courses developed within and for conventional adult education to programs that compete with for-profit institutions and corporate programs. These are often intentionally independent of regional processes for quality assurance. Standards for accreditation, relying on institutional self-study and peer review, serve as nationally and internationally accepted processes of quality assurance. This contextual framework has been the elaboration of institutional mission, educational programs, and student outcomes. Focused on traditional settings or conventional campus-based programs, regional accreditors are now compelled to conduct their own self-evaluation, renewing their commitment to cooperation among regions and reflecting on what constitutes quality in education for this new century.

Each of the six regional accrediting associations has begun a two-year process of reflection, with the goal of providing effective strategies for quality assurance that serves the complex array of educational institutions (McMurtrie, 2000). This twenty-four-month review is exceptionally rapid for organizations accustomed to the lengthier, more cautionary, and deliberative cycles of change. As distance-education providers invoke terms such as *university, faculty,* and *deans,* they strain the attributions used by accreditors and seen by the public as imparting credibility. It is the adoption of this mantle of "belonging to the academy" by the new providers that is one of many triggers for accreditors to seek a common definition of what constitutes quality in distance education that transcends the geography of their regional boundaries.

The six regional associations cooperated on a set of guidelines for the "evaluation of electronically offered degree and certificate programs." These guidelines offer a "system of accountability grounded in enduring values and principles through which quality has been defined" for what they term "responsible innovation" (Council of Regional Accrediting Commissions, 2000, p. iii). They represent explicit attention to the challenges posed by distance-education providers, bringing a convergence of various statements developed regionally since the 1990s.[9] The regional accreditation commissions for higher education will continue to limit their review to degree-granting institutions of higher learning; in doing so, they seek an unprecedented "degree of cross-regional consistency, compatible with their independence and autonomy," while also relying on current expectations that "nearly all on-line programming leading to degrees is being provided by traditional institutions which have a substantial academic infrastructure within a single region" (Council of Regional Accrediting Commissions, 2000, p. iii).

The adoption and implementation of the proposed September 2000 statement will draw on cross-regional cooperation. Such mutual aid was facilitated in part by the formation of CHEA in 1996 and by its sponsorship of two annual forums, Assuring Quality in Distance Learning. This mutual assistance among the regional associations builds on their individual guidelines, which since 1997 have adapted or incorporated distance-learning technology into existing standards (Middle States Association of Schools and Colleges, 1997, 1999; New England Association of Schools and Colleges, 1996; Western Association of Schools and Colleges, 1999). Some regional guidelines currently appear to pour the new wine of distance learning into the old bottle of recognition in that institutions must receive prior approval under the traditional procedure of "substantive change" before offering at least 50 percent of a degree program through distance learning. Significant concerns reflected the accreditors' desire for institutional commitment to resources, planning, faculty involvement, academic integrity, and assurances of student learning.

Changing Viewfinders: Seeing Distance-Learning Entities as Educational Institutions

The New England Association of Schools and Colleges (NEASC), the nation's oldest regional accrediting agency and the only one that serves institutions at all levels of education, recently attempted to distinguish distance learning from off-campus and alternative offerings. It identified distance-education programs as exceeding the earlier interpretation as another form of instruction or as an alternate instructional site for an institution (NEASC, 1996, 1997). Thus, the September 2000 statement of the Council of Regional Accrediting Commissions contributes a robust set of standards regarding the quality of education offered through distributed-learning environments, advancing more timid steps taken by individual accrediting agencies over conventional periods of time associated with the review of standards. For example, NEASC's "Principles of Good Practice for Electronically Offered Academic Degree and Certificate Programs" was not intended to replace the "Standards for Accreditation"; rather, the aim is to "give direction in the review of distance education programs as a part of the accreditation process" (New England Association of Schools and Colleges, 1996, p. 1). In its companion document, the NEASC definition of distance education was presented "as a formal educational process in which the majority of instruction occurs when student and instructor are not in the same place. Instruction may be synchronous or asynchronous. Distance education may employ correspondence study, or audio, video, or computer technologies" (New England Association of Schools and Colleges, 1997, p. 9).

This 1997 NEASC review was developed by a task force on distance education to address "all the concerns of the regional commissions on institutions of higher education" (p. 1), broadening the concerns found in the principles of the Western Interstate Commission on Higher Education endorsed by the regional associations a year earlier. The need to guide peer reviewer teams assessing the quality of distance education was clearly more pronounced and urgent than in 1977, when NEASC's Commission on Institutions of Higher Education reported to its board "that a major problem facing the Commission" was "how to handle agencies that are empowered to grant degrees, and yet operate without a faculty or campus" (New England Association of Schools and Colleges, 1986, p. 113). Distance education now invited greater attention by the accrediting associations, as exemplified by a 1998 focus issue of the *American Journal of Distance Education.*

States also have recognized the challenge posed by distance education to ensuring the quality of educational programs. Yet their responses also have been scattered rather than coherent. They often have adapted outmoded licensure or degree charter legislation to apply to the new virtual organizations. Considerable work remains on a legislative level as virtual universities seek authorization to operate within states that continue to refer to outdated criteria.[10]

Strange Bedfellows: Distance Education and Standards-Based Accreditation

Accreditation seeks what the Middle States Association of Colleges and Schools (1997) terms "clear processes to guide the educational policies that underpin the distance learning program and curricula" (p. 2). Specialists in campus computing, such as K. C. Green, urge caution about investing in new computer endeavors without ensuring that academic programs are improved as well. Policymakers and congressional leaders may find pressure to move the agenda from the current rush to provide equitable access to computers for students at all levels to insisting that the effectiveness of these efforts will be as measurable and subject to quality control. Thus, distance education may heighten the pressure on accrediting agencies to coordinate and develop assessment standards and guidelines that ask comparable questions, regardless of whatever mode of education is offered: What is your mission? Can you demonstrate that learning has occurred?

Faculty and public concern converge on the issue of credibility of the courses and programs offered on-line as well as on-campus. Efforts to ensure that effective learning occurs in either environment will be a net gain for both distance education and accreditation.

Over the past three decades, accreditors (and the public) have supported the rapid rise of distance education with little attention to new benchmarks for evaluation and assessment. We now must concern ourselves with the following issues or devalue the opportunities ahead:

Do institutional standards for higher education apply to distance learning by colleges and universities, as well as the new virtual providers?

Who will serve as the peer reviewers for the virtual universities?

How will standards be reformed to guide the quality education of distance learning?

What assumptions regarding certain aspects of the learning climate—such as class size, attendance, retention, degree completion, the provision of student services, and the mechanisms for dealing with academic transgressions—should be discarded or modified? For example, Harcourt.com accepts an eight-year cycle for baccalaureate completion. Most for-profit distance-education providers tolerate and accept a graduation or degree completion rate of 8 percent, noting that many of their students merely are seeking professional development courses.

Does the primary responsibility for the development and improvement of educational programs lie with faculty, as current accreditation guidelines typically state? Distance-education providers need to demonstrate that they enjoy full participation by the college community, employ faculty with appropriate professional qualifications, are responsible for the development and improvement of the instructional program, have a shared system of governance particularly with regard to academic affairs, and are evaluated to ensure they are effective in their work with students. How can or should these standards be reformed to serve distance-education providers?

Will students be ensured a balance or variety of instructional approaches (for example, will they still have a choice to take courses, on-line or traditional, that best meet their learning preferences)?

While high school and college on-line courses can be valuable to those otherwise unable to take specialized or advance placement offerings (such as those in rural schools or impoverished school regions), how will we ensure that learning has occurred and that students have been well served?

New Directions for Accrediting Associations

Jacob Ludes, chief executive officer of NEASC, acknowledges that the regional associations are challenged by new distance-education providers that have assumed the mantle and nomenclature of traditional higher education. He sees this as an opportunity for the regional associations to renew their commitment to mutual cooperation in applying their frameworks and standards to develop a common definition of what constitutes quality in distance education (Ludes, 2000a). Distance-education providers' focus on "customizing education" for their clientele is similar to that of Web-based entrepreneurs who "look for a big, inefficient market that could be radically transformed" (Dell, 2000, p. 9). According to Ludes, "Accrediting associations rely on the historical success of providing coherent and sustained application of the self-evaluation process to improve and strengthen education" (Ludes, 2000a).

The accrediting associations' response to distance education will require "meaningful institutional involvement in developing standards that are more broad in defining the practice of accreditation" (Ludes, 2000a). In February 2001, the eight commissions of higher education that form the Council of Regional Accrediting Commissions will act on their September 2000 Statement on the Evaluation of Electronically Offered Degrees. According to Ludes (2000a), their action is likely to reflect that the distance-education program should:

Be consistent with the institution's role and mission, identifying the extent to which it remains in compliance or represents substantial change that triggers prior review and approval processes.

Be supported by an appropriate commitment of institutional budget (including technical, physical plant, staff, and technical assistance) and policy statements that support student program completion.

Rely on an organization structure that offers adequate support for program implementation, including adequate and appropriate relationships to academic structure.

Strive to ensure a consistent and coherent technical framework for articulation and transfer of course and programs, as well as a framework for students and faculty.

Provide technical support for students in a variety of schemas, including on-line and person-to-person contact.

Choose technologies appropriate to the requirements of programs, curricula, and students served.

Observe requirements of regional and federal jurisdictions, including those related to disabilities, copyright law, state and national requirements for postsecondary institutions, and dissemination of sensitive information or technologies.

Allow curricula to evolve consistent with the discipline, but also allow standards of quality to endure, relying heavily on qualified faculty and a focus on learning outcomes for an increasingly diverse student population.

Conclusion: Ensuring a "Net Gain"

Accrediting associations should be applauded for examining the new realities created by a myriad of distance-education providers. Technology-mediated distance learning will transform the learning landscape on campus and on-line. Accreditors will need to consider what accommodations are necessary in order for them to continue to serve as a credible authority on the quality of education provided. We conclude with a list of issues we believe must be addressed in order to allow this inquiry to reinvigorate the self-evaluation process:

Accrediting associations and distance-education providers must define mutually acceptable options for program recognition so each may continue to play a valuable role in the provision of higher education. Akin to the recent collision of interests among environmentalists and loggers in the Pacific Northeast, accrediting associations and distance-education providers must each negotiate to ensure their future role.

Caution should be exercised to ensure that alternative assessment practices do not result in a diminution of program-specific standards. To what extent will or should accreditors focus on outcomes without examining content of curricula, whether on-line or on-campus?

Although the nation's accrediting associations prepare to launch much-needed guidelines for distance-education programs, they will also need to develop guidelines for off-site institutions. The proposed guidelines are for site-based higher education institutions engaged in distance learning. They will either form the basis for the accreditation of virtual universities or clarify why they cannot.

Distance-education providers should reflect on their perceived need for and the effects of seeking regional accreditation. What value should they place on this accepted process of self-evaluation and assessment? How accommodating are they willing to be to those standards?

Both distance-education providers and accrediting associations need to recognize that their autonomy may be affected as the federal government expands its scrutiny of the quality of educational programs and seeks to confirm program validity for the public.

The reality is that higher education is traveling along a far less familiar path. Technological innovation is the primary instigator of the rapid evolution of postsecondary and adult education, but other inputs, such as increased competition and interest, have stimulated interest beyond that of academia. The corporate world now looks to higher education as an opportunity ripe for the picking.

During the latter half of the 1990s, accreditors began asking the difficult questions about how to deal with the growing distance-education market. These questions are complex, as are the answers. The difficulty for IHEs and other educational providers will be in making appropriate changes in quality control while the technology and pedagogy change under their feet. This alone argues for a set of standards and practices based on indicators that allow for flexibility in terms of delivery.

Distance education and mediated learning are here to stay. Both higher education and the public are cognizant of that fact. The good news is that higher education has begun to deal with these issues head-on. The challenge will be to keep future discussion focused on quality rather than gatekeeping.

Notes

1. See www.essentialschools.org for further information.

2. The Fathom.com consortium includes Columbia University, the Smithsonian's National Museum of Natural History, the New York Public Library, the London School of Economics, Cambridge University Press, and the British Library. This new Internet company will invest $80 million in 2000–2001 alone, will distribute information, and will offer on-line classes to users around the world.

3. See www.HarcourtHigherEd.com.

4. Information technology certification programs, unlike programs found in education, do not necessarily include an instructional provider. Although they are not the focus of this chapter, they too demand quality assurance at a time when certification programs have exploded in number. Adelman (2000) notes that the majority of these programs are based in subbaccalaureate institutions and are more likely found as continuing- or extended-education units of these four-year not-for-profits. Even as these are likely to remain at "the periphery of higher education," the U.S. Department of Education produced a report (1999) comparing a new system of credentialing for the information technology and telecommunications industries since 1990 to that used by traditional higher education.

5. Some regional accrediting associations prefer to offer alternative accreditation processes, such as the Academic Quality Improvement Project of the North Central Association of Schools and Colleges, as a desirable approach for institutions already accredited (Crow, 2000). Also see www.aqip.com.

6. Although this chapter pertains to higher education, the issues apply to elementary and secondary education as well. High schools increasingly are moving from subscribing to individual on-line courses to joining virtual high school consortia (such as the Concord Consortium). Absent accrediting standards for entirely virtual institutions at any grade level, public, private, and international schools rapidly may make an end run around accreditation. For example, the popularity of on-line virtual college tours has led businesses such as entrepreneurial U.S. News to pilot plans for Web-based admissions counseling "to simplify the process of getting into college but also remove some of the stress by making it fun." For example, "a computer personality test that is designed to match students to campuses doesn't ask about SAT scores, but rather whether a student likes to ski or comb the beach" (Brownstein, 2000).

7. The eight higher education commissions of the six regional accrediting associations will discuss and review the September 17, 2000, report, *Statement of the Regional Accrediting Commissions on the Evaluation of Electronically Offered Degree and Certificate Programs, and Guidelines for the Evaluation of Electronically Offered Degree and Certificate Programs,* at its February 2001 meeting. These commissions and associations are the commissions on higher education of the Middle States Association of Colleges and Schools and the New England Association of Schools and Colleges, the North Central Association of Schools and Colleges, the Northwest Association of Schools and Colleges, the Southern Association of Colleges and Schools, the Accrediting Commission for Senior Colleges, and the Accrediting Commission for Community and Junior Colleges of the Western Association of Schools and Colleges.

8. See www.wiche.edu/telecom.

9. The September 2000 document serves as a draft for a 2001 report, which is available from the regional associations or the Council for Higher Education Accreditation.

10. Regulations for charter schools require revamping to incorporate the delivery of distance education. State legislatures and state education agencies need to examine such regulations prior to, rather than in response to, applications by distance-education providers. Charter school adherence to state regulations must precede accreditation candidacy.

References

Adelman, C. *A Parallel Postsecondary Universe: The Certification System in Information Technology.* Washington, D.C.: Office of Educational Research and Improvement, U.S. Department of Education, 2000.

Brownstein, A. "U.S. News Apologizes for Secretly Filming Focus Group on Proposed Mobile Counseling Center." *Chronicle of Higher Education,* Oct. 24, 2000.

Chronicle of Higher Education. "Letters to the Editors." Oct. 27, 2000, p. B17.

Council of Regional Accrediting Commissions. "Statement of the Regional Accrediting Commissions on the Evaluation of Electronically Offered Degree and Certificate Programs, and Guidelines for the Evaluation of Electronically Offered Degree and Certificate Programs." Washington, D.C.: Council of Regional Accrediting Commissions, Sept. 17, 2000.

Crow, S. "To the Editor." *Chronicle of Higher Education,* Oct. 27, 2000, p. B17.

Dell, M. "Big M2000.com: E-commerce and the Enterprise." *MIT Tech Talk,* Oct. 18, 2000, p. 9.

Green, K. C. *Struggling with IT Staffing.* Encino, Calif.: Campus Computing Project, Oct. 2000.

Harcourt Higher Education. *Undergraduate Catalog 2000–2001.* Cambridge, Mass.: Harcourt Higher Education, 2000.

Institute for Higher Education Policy. *Quality on the Line: Benchmarks for Success in Internet-Based Distance Education.* Washington, D.C.: Institute for Higher Education Policy, 2000.

Investor's Business Daily (2000, March 29). "Online Learning Moves to Head of Class," p. A8.

Jones, G. *Cyberschools.* Englewood, Colo.: Jones Digital Century, 1977.

Lezberg, A. K. "Quality Control in Distance Education: The Role of Regional Accreditation." *American Journal of Distance Education,* 1998, *12*(2), 26–35.

Ludes, J. (2000a, September 11). Personal interview conducted by authors.

Ludes, J. *President's Report to Trustees of NEASC.* Unpublished internal document. Bedford, Mass.: New England Association of Schools and Colleges, Sept. 14, 2000.

McMurtrie, B. "Accreditors Revamp Policies to Stress Student Learning." *Chronicle of Higher Education,* July 7, 2000.

Marchese, T. "Not-So-Distant Competitors: How New Providers Are Remaking the Postsecondary Marketplace." *AAHE Bulletin,* 50(9), 3–7, 1998.

Middle States Association of Schools and Colleges, Commission on Higher Education. *Guidelines for Distance Learning Programs.* Philadelphia: Taskforce on Distance Learning, 1997.

Middle States Association of Schools and Colleges, Commission on Higher Education. *Addendum to Designs for Excellence, Standards of Accreditation.* Philadelphia: Middle States Association of Schools and Colleges, 1999.

New England Association of Schools and Colleges. *The First Hundred Years, 1885–1985, New England Association of Schools and Colleges.* Bedford, Mass.: New England Association of Schools and Colleges, 1986.

New England Association of Schools and Colleges, Commission on Higher Education. *Principles of Good Practice for Electronically Offered Academic Degree and Certificate Programs.* Bedford, Mass.: New England Association of Schools and Colleges, Nov. 1996.

New England Association of Schools and Colleges, Commission on Higher Education. *Proposed Policy and Procedures for the Review of Distance Education Activities.* Bedford, Mass.: New England Association of Schools and Colleges, Sept. 18, 1997.

NUA. "How Many Online?" [www.nua.net/surveys/how_many_online/index.html]. 2000.

U.S. Department of Education. *Distance Education at Postsecondary Education Institutions: 1997–98.* Washington, D.C.: U.S. Government Printing Office, 1999.

Wellman, J. V. "Accreditors Have to See Past 'Learning Outcomes.'" *Chronicle of Higher Education,* Sept. 22, 2000.

Western Association of Schools and Colleges, Accrediting Commission for Community and Junior Colleges. *Handbook on Distance Learning.* Santa Rosa, Calif.: Western Association of Schools and Colleges, July 1999.

WATSON SCOTT SWAIL is senior policy analyst at SRI International in Arlington, Virginia, and former associate director of policy analysis for The College Board in Washington, D.C.

EVA KAMPITS is director of the Office of School/College Relations, New England Association of Schools and Colleges.

4

The case of teacher education accreditation is a microcosm of higher education accreditation and assessment writ large. Can accreditation serve both accountability and improvement agenda, and can assessment deliver its claims about graduates' competence?

From Consensus Standards to Evidence of Claims: Assessment and Accreditation in the Case of Teacher Education

Frank Brush Murray

Over time accreditation, which initially met the narrow need for a college or university to convince other institutions that its students and courses should be accepted by them, and vice versa, evolved to provide assurances to those outside the higher education community, as well as those inside it, that the institution had the capacity to offer its programs. As it developed, accreditation became one of three major mechanisms that a higher education institution could use to persuade the public that it deserved to be considered and treated like the nation's other colleges and universities.

The other two mechanisms were government regulation, requiring compliance with government mandates, laws, rules, and statutes that regulated and defined higher education, and competition, yielding success in the higher education marketplace to those institutions that had more of the attractive attributes that define higher education institutions and to those who market and promote these institutions.

Because the regulation mechanisms concentrate on compliance and the competition mechanisms on public relations and marketability, both of which are linked to institutional capacity, the accreditation mechanism has been freed somewhat from its traditional and exclusive focus on capacity to focus on the integrity of the academic program and increases in its quality.

Graham, Lyman, and Trow (1995) argued, however, that even here the prevailing system of voluntary accreditation in the United States as it evolved is fundamentally flawed because it grew into a system with two simultaneous and incompatible functions:

The improvement of an institution's performance based on its continual assessment and evaluation of its strengths and weaknesses
The certification and assurance to the public of the soundness of the institution's practices

The second function invariably overwhelms the first because the incentives favor the production of a public relations document that magnifies the institution's strengths and hides its weaknesses. This is precisely the opposite of what is needed if the first function is to be served.

The accreditation of teacher education provides an instructive case of how these two incompatible factors can be brought into balance through a greater reliance on the assessment of student learning than has been evident in accreditation systems until now. The integration of evidence about student learning into the accreditation process, however, introduces complexities and difficulties that radically alter the process.

Some Unique Characteristics of the Teaching Profession

Teaching is seemingly different from the other learned professions on several interrelated dimensions. By comparison with other professions, it is massive (3 million members compared with law's 400,000, for example) and less well compensated. There are, for example, approximately 1,300 schools of education in contrast to 180 law schools and 125 medical schools. In teaching, unlike most other professions, the client does most of the work (the students labor to learn their lessons, but the lawyer's clients can do very little on their own to produce justice). Unlike other professions, teachers do not set or control the standards for their profession. The skills of the teaching profession, in contrast to the skills of the other professions, seem quite accessible to laypersons. Nearly every adult teaches someone something in the course of daily life and believes he or she could teach school but simply does not want to. Indeed, teaching is seen as a natural act that is readily observed in those who have had no professional tutoring in the profession of teaching. Moreover, professional training in teaching is apparently not very difficult, because unlike the other professions, persons of modest abilities are admitted to teacher education programs, and few of them fail. In fact, almost all earn top marks for their efforts.

Quality Assurance in the Teaching Profession

Not one of the standard mechanisms for the assurance of quality has the result for the teaching profession that it apparently has for the other professions. While the teaching profession, like the other professions, has licenses, certificates, academic degrees, accreditation, standardized examinations, standards boards, and so forth, their outcomes seem afflicted, at least in the public mind, with more false-positive mistakes than in the other professions. The public and policymakers, in other words, have come to doubt that the traditional methods of ensuring quality in teaching yield what they seem able to yield elsewhere. They believe that many teachers with licenses, academic degrees from accredited schools of education, certificates, and so forth are not competent in their work (Conant, 1963; Koerner, 1963; Judge, Lemosse, Paine, and Sedlak, 1994).

As a result, all but ten states have added basic skill tests to the license requirements. The subject matter of the tests (four-function arithmetic, spelling, basic reading comprehension) ordinarily would be a presumed prerequisite to the college degree. Thirty states retest the graduate's subject matter knowledge, presumably because the college major or the degree in education is an insufficient indicator of competence in the teaching field. The recent reauthorization of the federal Higher Education Act does not permit funds to go to a college or school of education, preferring instead that the education school partner with the "more responsible" public schools or arts and science colleges. So that the public can have assurances not provided by the education degree or by accreditation, section 211 of Title II of the Higher Education Act requires that only colleges of education (not business, law, medicine, physical therapy, or nursing schools) report the pass rate of their graduates on state licensing examinations. Fewer than half the nation's education schools and colleges of education are accredited, a fact that may have no appreciable consequence for a school's reputation or for the prospects for its graduates. This fact would not be troubling if only the worst schools of education were unaccredited, but some of the leading and nationally ranked schools of education have declined the opportunity to be accredited. Apparently neither accreditation of the schools of education nor the degrees they offer seem to provide a trustworthy basis for professional practice. This depressing trend does not stop here, however.

The National Board for Professional Teaching Standards (NBPTS) elected not to require a degree in teacher education or a teaching license for those permitted to sit for its certification examinations. Alternative routes to the state's teaching license, increasingly popular with policymakers, invariably bypass the teacher education degree. Even when based on graduation from a teacher education program, state requirements for teaching licenses are easily waived, and the licenses are typically not required for private school. It would be an unthinkable public policy to require driving licenses only for those who drive publicly owned vehicles or medical licenses only for those who work in public hospitals and clinics. However, policymakers have required that only teachers employed in public settings be licensed. Also, states regularly grant the teaching license to graduates of unaccredited schools, a practice without parallel in law or medicine. It is rare indeed to find tangible evidence that anyone—inside or outside the profession—has confidence that the education school degree, the teaching license, or the accreditation status of the education school can be trusted to accomplish what they seem to accomplish in other fields.

Replacing Standards for *Doing No Harm* with Standards for Excellence

By and large, it is assumed that professionals are so invested in their sense of integrity and expertise that the public good is protected and promoted if professionals are given license to act on their specialized knowledge in behalf of their clients (Meier, 2000). Only the most minimal external standards and regulations are needed in these circumstances to protect the public, and these regulations are only to ensure that the professional inadvertently or, in rare cases, deliberately does no harm.

In the immediate post–*Nation at Risk* (National Commission on Excellence in Education, 1983) period, two groups concluded that these *do no harm* standards were insufficient. In fact, they would likely perpetuate and increase the poor educational performance of the nation's schools and school children. The Carnegie Corporation of New York and the Holmes Group felt that the standards of the day, if continued, would guarantee that teaching would never be like the other learned professions. Both sought remedies through the invention and formulation of standards for excellence: standards that defined the kind of superior professional performance that would end the nation's risk and place teaching on a par with the other professions.

The Carnegie Forum on Education and the Economy (1996) concluded that a national board for professional teaching standards was needed to develop and define national standards for master teachers and create a political impetus to encourage teachers and school districts to reach these high standards. These standards were meant to go beyond the *do no harm* standards for licensure that all teachers meet. These were standards that defined excellent or world-class teaching.

At the same time, a committee of education deans from the Association of Deans of Land Grant Universities grappled with the standards that education schools should meet for accreditation. The committee agreed first to take up the question of the *do no harm* standards for education schools that would be analogous to the standards that states used for the teaching license. The committee concluded that a redesigned National Council for the Accreditation of Teacher Education would satisfy the need for the minimum accreditation standards—those below which a school of education should not be permitted to operate. For a number of reasons, largely internal to the organization, the committee did not go on to address the second issue: the formulation of standards that would define superior or world-class schools of education. Some of the deans, however, did pursue the second question independently, and their deliberations led to the formation of the Holmes Group.

Ninety-six American research universities formed the Holmes Group in 1987 and committed themselves to improve the quality of schooling through research and development and the preparation of professional teachers. They set out five goals, two of which foreshadowed current reforms in teacher education accreditation:

• *Make teaching intellectually sound.* The Holmes Group wanted prospective teachers to have a broad, coherent liberal arts foundation that incorporated enduring multicultural values and forms of inquiry, and they wanted it taught to a depth of understanding that enabled teachers to teach well. They sought to present the study and practice of teaching in a coherent sequence of courses (liberal arts, education studies, and clinical experiences) that integrated research findings about learning and teaching and demonstrated how to select and shape particular content knowledge into clear, challenging lessons for all children and adolescents.[1]

They did not prescribe, incidentally, that the start of professional studies must be delayed until graduate school. Nor did they propose that new teachers must have a master's degree before being recommended for a teaching license. They did not prescribe a structure for teacher education, but did commit to making professional preparation programs the central mission of the school of education. This entailed a critical rethinking of the existing content of professional programs. It meant working with liberal arts professors and practicing teachers and administrators to devise a program that was academically and professionally solid and integrated.

• *Create relevant and intellectually defensible standards of entry into teaching.* The Holmes Group saw the need to develop multiple evaluation instruments, measuring diverse kinds of competence, for use at several stages: admittance to teacher education, admittance to student teaching and internship in a school, and the recommendation for a teaching license. They saw that the available standardized tests and licensing exams were minimalist tests that had little value in predicting the future performance of beginning teachers. These tests did not guarantee the public of a teacher's capability to teach, nor did these exams indicate how well a teacher education program prepared teachers.

More Recent Proposals

Despite the decades of conscientious redesign and reform efforts by the Holmes Group and the National Board for Professional Teaching Standards, the National Commission on Teaching and America's Future (NCTAF) in its 1996 report, *What Matters Most: Teaching for America's Future,* concluded that the country was not "serious about standards" and that American teacher education and professional development required "reinvention." NCTAF proposed a strategy to remedy the problems associated with teacher education and the low performance of America's teachers and students. It was a three-pronged effort to raise standards for the teaching license, the accreditation of schools of education, and the performance of tenured teachers.

The NCTAF proposal required a settled professional knowledge base.[2] However, many would find the knowledge base on which the standards would be established less steady and certain than would be needed to justify the political imposition of these standards on large numbers of students, teachers, and institutions.[3]

The standards on which the recommendations were based (those of the National Board for Professional Teaching Standards, the Interstate New Teacher Assessment and Support Consortium, and the National Council for the Accreditation of Teacher Education) are all under development and, promising as they are, they have not been validated.[4] They are provisional, empirically untested, and built only on an emerging consensus of well-intentioned leading professional educators. It is entirely possible that a school of education could meet them and the public would still not know whether the candidates for the degree had mastered critical knowledge and skill, whether the faculty's assessment system of that knowledge and skill was valid, and whether the faculty had based its decisions on evidence from a quality control system that could locate weaknesses in the program.

In 1996, the newly formed Teacher Education Accreditation Council (TEAC) proposed an alternative solution to the current practice of accrediting schools of education by their conformity to consensus standards. The TEAC proposal addressed the quality control system the teacher education faculty has in place and the quality of the evidence that the system yields about the accomplishments of the teacher education degree programs (see Dill, Massy, Williams, and Cook, 1996; Graham, Lyman, and Trow, 1995; Trow, 1998). More important, it required that the evidence be solid and convincing about the one element that is currently in doubt about today's teacher education programs: whether the graduates in fact had acquired the knowledge, disposition, and skill their academic degrees indicate and that the state license requires (Teacher Education Accreditation Council, 1999).

Traditionally, accreditation is a peer review and evaluation of the institution's capacity to be a college or university—whether it possesses the characteristics and the capacities that define a college or university. In the case of specialized accreditation, the question is whether the unit meets certain consensus standards and criteria that indicate that it is a college or school of education. TEAC was primarily concerned with another issue: what the program faculty did with that capacity in teacher education and whether it had solid, credible evidence to back up its claims for what it did.

TEAC, in other words, answered different questions—questions more about the program than the institution. Is there a credible reason to believe the faculty has actually accomplished what it thinks it has accomplished, how does it know, and is the evidence strong enough to convince disinterested experts?

Because so many leading and highly ranked schools of education have not participated in the current system of accreditation, it is reasonable to reexamine how professional education programs are accredited and try a new approach to accreditation. TEAC's new system is proving to be attractive to institutions with sound programs because it yields evidence on which the faculty can make better decisions and respond effectively to their poorly informed critics, whose complaints invariably rely on tainted evidence.[5]

The Nature of the Evidence

If the knowledge base is too weak to support standards, as TEAC and others claim (Meier, 2000; Ohanian, 1999, 2000; Raths, 1999), it is fair to ask if the nature and validity of the evidence and scholarship in the field of teacher education are equal to the task of assuring the public that its teachers are well educated and competent.

Validity refers to the appropriateness, uses, and quality of the faculty's interpretations of the results of the assessment system it has in place. It requires considerations of the dependability, persuasiveness, and trustworthiness of several kinds of evidence—evidence about the content of the assessments, assessment-criterion relationships, the theoretical and scholarly basis of the construct being assessed, and the consequences of the assessments.[6]

For all practical purposes, today's program faculty can typically provide evidence of student learning by some combination of the following items, each of which is plagued with known flaws and distortions:

1. Student grades and grade-point averages in each component of the program (subject matter, liberal arts, pedagogy, teaching skill)
2. Portfolios of representative academic accomplishments and work samples in the areas of the program
3. Student scores on standardized license examinations in any of the areas of the program
4. Student scores on admission tests for graduate study in the areas of the program
5. Job placement rates (particularly those indicating that the students were first-choice applicants)
6. Program completion rates
7. Evaluations by employers of program graduates' professional performance with regard to the program areas, especially teaching competence
8. Alumni follow-up studies with regard to the components of the program
9. Professional recognition rates of graduates (awards, prizes, Board recognition, and other accomplishments of note) that are based on the elements of the program
10. Rates of professional advanced study (graduate degrees, diplomas, additional teaching certificates) in the areas of the program

11. Rates of professional advancement of program graduates (for example, promotions, leadership roles) that are related to the areas of the program
12. Rates of professional activities related to the program (such as authoring textbooks and curriculum materials, participating in standard setting and monitoring commissions, in-service instructor roles, higher education teaching, scholarly publications, professional development school assignments)
13. Academic achievements of the program graduates (pupil grades, standardized scores and gains, and other measures of academic accomplishment)
14. Case studies of candidates' learning and accomplishment in the areas of the program[7]
15. Work samples from practice teachers' teaching in which the lesson or unit and the results of the instruction are documented with regard to key areas of the program

There are serious but manageable validity issues within each of these categories of evidence. For example, hiring rates in times of teacher shortages may not be the indicator of student accomplishment that they would have been in times of teacher oversupply. In times of shortage, hiring rates may indicate nothing about quality, but the rate of first-choice hired applicants, for example, may prove to be a valid indicator of student accomplishment. Similarly, items on rates of professional recognition, professional advanced study, professional advancement, and professional activities may be relatively meaningless if the rates are low or less than the normative rates. The rates may indicate something important about the program's quality, however, if they are significantly higher than the norm. Passing rates on the currently available teaching license tests, for example, are surprisingly high, but the passing scores are set at the twenty-fifth percentile of actual cohort performance and with fewer than half the test's items answered correctly in some cases (Mitchell and Barth, 1999).

Course grades are meant to be a measure of subject matter understanding, but their validity is threatened by the fact that they are frequently measures of other matters that may have only a tangential or no relationship to the student's mastery of the subject matter of the course. Some of the common threats to the validity of course grades occur when they become influenced by other factors and become, as a result, measures of these other factors. In contemporary higher education, it is fair to say that grades may be, in varying degrees, measures of any, or all, of the following:

A measure of punctuality (when faculty take points off for late work or give extra points for early work)
A measure of gain or growth (when faculty base the grade on the degree of improvement over the course of the semester)

A measure of place in a distribution (when faculty assign grades on the curve or some predetermined percentage formula so that the grades only indicate students' percentile or rank in the class)

A measure of dishonesty (when faculty or the university lower the grade for cheating or plagiarism, with the result that a low grade is uninterpretable because it may signify a low level of understanding or a low level of honesty)

A measure of extra or additional achievement (when faculty give extra points for more work that may not be qualitatively superior to the prior work but is simply quantitatively more than other students have done)

A measure of attendance (when faculty deduct points for cutting class)

A measure of writing skill (or some prior expertise separable from the subject matter as when neatness, rhetoric, or format counts)

A measure of reduced spread (when faculty inflate the grades or reduce the variance as in the quip, "The best way to turn C students into B students is to put them in graduate school")

A measure of motivation and perseverance (when students receive the last grade of several unsuccessful attempts at the subject matter or when effort is rewarded)

A measure of student background (when faculty members introduce examples and analogies that speak to some groups of students more than others, or when there is cultural bias in the teaching format)[7]

A measure of political statement (when faculty are sensitive to the student's draft or immigration status, scholarship and grant conditions, graduate or undergraduate status, and gender, and take these into consideration in the assignment of course grades)

Thus, we are left with a cluster of measures, each flawed and weak. However, if taken together, they may converge and align and constitute an improved evidentiary base for the program faculty's claim that the program's graduates are competent. This evidentiary base is more direct than the consensus standards approach, which in the past would have anchored, for example, the evidence of student learning in the course syllabus.[8]

The Evolution of Evidence

The evolution of evidence we have available is slow. For example, after the *Nation at Risk* report (National Commission on Teaching and America's Future, 1996), the U.S. secretary of education posted a wall chart representing the educational health of each state by its mean Scholastic Aptitude Test (SAT) score (or American College Test score). The validity of the evidence was low partly because it was not corrected for participation rates (the number and portion of the population taking the test), which had a significant impact on the mean scores (the greater the participation, the lower was the mean). Even corrected for participation, the mean SAT was an imperfect, although readily available, measure, because the test had been designed to be insensitive to the variations in the high school curriculum. The SAT, an ability test, gradually has been replaced as a measure of educational health in public policy discourse in favor of the National Assessment of Educational Progress (NAEP) tests, which were actually about the curriculum. However, until federal legislation regarding the use of NAEP was modified, state norms could not be reported or compared. The shift from the SAT to NAEP, while requiring decades, was largely a change in political wisdom and strategy. Shifts that are based on evolving scholarship, such as are needed for valid measures of teacher competence, require even longer periods and complex analysis.

Consider the kind of evidence we would accept as conclusively indicating that a child knows the simple school concept that the number remains the same when the configuration of five objects becomes spread out. What would the child have to say or do to convince us that she knew what we know: that the number is the same even though the spread-out row looks as if there were objects? This would appear to be a simple matter, far less demanding than what we would need to ask of a prospective teacher to determine teaching competence. We would ask the child whether the number in the spread-out row was more than, less than, or the same as the number in the original row and take the child's answer as a solid indicator of what the child understood about number and spatial arrangement.

What has frustrated researchers, who were initially inclined to pose and rely on such a question, was that young children (and some adults confronted with more complex arrangements of objects) would argue, even after correctly counting the number, that the spread-out row still had more objects. What did the child's assertion of inequality mean? What was it evidence of? A problem in the child's perception, language, cognition, maturation, learning, development, logic, or something else?

The methods that would yield conclusive evidence to this question have taken over thirty years (from the 1960s to the 1990s) to analyze and assemble (Murray, 1978, 1990, 1992; Smith, 1993). They have the following eight elements that are emblematic of the work still to be done in the field of teacher education:

1. *Judgment.* What the child says in response to the question, Does this row have more than, less than, or the same number as the other row?
2. *Reasons.* The child might support the assertion of equality with appeals to the fact that nothing was added or subtracted, that there were the same objects in the row, that the spread-out row could be put back as it was before, that one row only looks as if there is more than the other, and so on. Whether these are adequate reasons is itself a matter of debate, but clearly we would want more than the child's response to the question in item 1, whatever it was.
3. *Duration.* Our confidence would increase if the child responded the same way at a later time on the assumption that ideas truly understood

are almost never given up, while those held on other grounds often fade.

4. *Resistance to countersuggestion.* On the assumption that what is truly understood is not easily modifiable, the child could be presented with counterevidence, pressure, and argument in an effort to change the child's response to see if she would give up her initial response.

5. *Specific transfer.* Our confidence that the child truly understood the number concept would increase if the assessment were made with different materials and with different tasks of the same specific form on the assumption that the understanding of number transcends any particular task features.

6. *Nonspecific transfer.* Our confidence in the evidence might increase further if the child succeeded in a family of tasks in different domains that had a common theoretical structure. If the child also knew that other features of numbers of objects (their mass or weight) were unaffected by spatial reorganization, we might be even more confident that the child truly understood the original number task.

7. *Trainability.* This criterion for understanding is the converse of the countersuggestion criterion since it assumes that a quick or abrupt change in response accuracy after feedback, hints, cues, argument, and so on indicates that the original response was not a valid indicator of true understanding. Because genuine understanding is a relatively slow process and not amenable to fast change, we assume that a quickly trained response is not based on genuine understanding. If the child were incorrect initially but was easily trained in the right answer, we would assume that the child really understood the problem all along, and that her initial failure was due to inattention or misinformation about some aspects of the task.

8. *Necessity.* If the child truly understood the task, she would also know that the outcome had to be what it was and could not be different from what it is, and so on. Our confidence increases further still should the child assert that the number is not only equal, but that it would always be equal and would never be affected by the spatial arrangement of the elements.

When all eight measures align themselves in a consistent pattern, we can be sure that the child truly understands what we understand about the number of objects in the array. If it proves so difficult to establish compelling evidence about such a simple matter as a child's concept of number and if the available methods of documenting a teacher's competence are of limited validity, how might we expect evidence in this domain to evolve and develop to the point that it could serve as a reliable basis for accreditation?

One promising line of thinking on this question can be found in an examination of Table 4.1, which gives the percentile scores of school children in Tennessee on the grade 5 standardized test of mathematics achievement as a function of whether the students were taught in grades 1 through 3 by

Table 4.1. Percentile Achievement in Grade 5 Mathematics in Two Tennessee School Systems

School System	Pathways through Grades 1–3 with Low-, Average-, and High-Gain Teachers						
Grade 1	Low	Low	Low	Average	Average	Average	High
Grade 2	Low	Low	Low	Average	Average	Average	High
Grade 3	Low	Average	High	Low	Average	High	High
School system A	44	63	83	61	80	92	96
School system B	29	40	59	39	50	70	83

Tests administered were the CTM/McGraw Tests

teachers who produced low, average, or high gains from their pupils (based on Sanders and Rivers, 1996, and Wright, Horn, and Sanders, 1997).

The data in the table indicate that teachers make substantial differences in student achievement, a point that has been in doubt since the 1960s, when differences in student achievement were attributed to differences in social class and other nonschool factors (Ferguson, 1991). The data reveal that if two pupils of equal standing and ability had entered school system A or B at the same time and one had three successive teachers who produced low gains in their pupils and the other had three successive teachers who produced high gains in their pupils, their fifth-grade math achievement would differ by 50 percentile points, a life-altering difference that seems wholly attributable to their respective teachers. Throughout the table, the data reveal that a teacher's beneficial or harmful influence extends over several years.

If it were the case that a school of education could show that the graduates of its elementary school teacher education program were overrepresented among the teachers who produced high gains and underrepresented among the teachers who produced low gains, we would take that as solid evidence of the program's success. Such evidence, in fact, would trump any evidence from the fifteen items of evidence categories. Few education programs at this time have access to the kind of evidence set out in Table 4.1, let alone the capacity to determine how their graduates figured in it. As the field evolves, however, this kind of evidence could become a staple in the case a faculty makes that its teacher education graduates are competent teachers. Moreover, it could form the basis of an accreditation decision in a system like the one TEAC has designed.

The Place of Accreditation Evidence

A large part of the problem with accreditation and the other quality assurance measures is that the teaching profession has not grounded its work in scholarly evidence. TEAC's accreditation system centers on the academic degree program and the system the program faculty use to satisfy themselves and others that their claims that their students are competent, caring, and qualified educators are warranted, can withstand scrutiny, and otherwise meet the tests and standards of scholarly evidence. NCATE 2000 also seeks to ground the accreditation decision in evidence that the education school's graduates can teach effectively.

This evidence is only one piece of the puzzle, however—a piece that speaks only to whether the students learned what the program faculty taught them about critical professional knowledge, disposition, and skill. The evidence that TEAC-accredited programs, for example, will have for their claims, while sound and a marked advance over typical accreditation practice, is likely to be inconclusive about whether a particular degree holder should teach. The public's confidence in the quality of its professional educators must rest on multiple and converging lines of evidence about the quality of the individuals who wish to teach. Accreditation provides only one of these several lines of evidence.

The other lines of evidence must come from independent assessments by others of different aspects of the prospective educator's competence. The states must secure independent evidence to warrant the granting of a license, school boards must secure their own evidence with regard to the hiring and the tenure decisions, standards boards must secure their own evidence to justify the granting of certificates, professional societies must devise their own kinds of evidence for the award of prizes and trophies, and so forth.

Because all the known measures and sources of evidence are subject to documented distortions and flaws, it is critical that the public have independent lines of evidence on the various aspects of educators' competencies—whether they have studied and mastered what matters most, whether they are entitled to a license, whether they should be hired and tenured, whether they deserve merit payments, promotions, and awards, and so on.

The key point is that there be solid evidence, grounded in the professional literature and standards of scholarship, to warrant the granting of degrees, licenses, certificates, professional positions, tenure, merit payments, promotions, and awards. TEAC's reform initiative, while purposefully limited to the evidence about the academic degree, applies with equal force to the work of all other constituents of the profession.

The prerequisite to the rise of the public's confidence in its professional educators is the quality of the evidence the other parties of the profession have for the decisions entrusted to them by the public. When these independent lines of evidence converge and agree with each other, the public will have confidence that we have the right person in the school. At that time their confidence will also be justified.

Lessons for the Accreditation of Other Professional Programs

The case of teacher education accreditation is a microcosm of higher education accreditation writ large. It is very difficult, for example, to find those who think that American higher education, whether accredited or not, is living up to the trust and confidence the public has invested in it (see Blits, 1985, for example). While the reputations of all civic institutions that are traditionally held in public trust have eroded, the charge against higher education is that it is not delivering on its promises. Students fail to receive the individual attention and guidance to which they and their tuition-paying parents thought they were entitled; they have not learned or understood what their grades indicate they have learned; legislators see fewer and fewer services to the state and community for each year's tax dollar subsidy; governors see the universities focused solely on a narrow research agenda that is unresponsive to the needs of the wider community; and alumni see that standards for academic degrees and honors have slipped to embarrassingly low levels. Accredited institutions, in particular, are seen as excessively costly and self-serving while failing to meet their obligations and promises. In the view of the most severe critics, the college degree has merely replaced the high school diploma of the 1950s in function and quality, and the mechanism of accreditation, as currently implemented, has not significantly altered these critics' view of the erosion of standards in higher education.

There are preliminary signs that the other learned professions may come to receive the kind of second-guessing treatment that thus far has been reserved for teachers. Physicians increasingly are seeing their professional judgments, warranted by their academic degrees, subordinated to decisions made by health managers. Judges are finding their professional judgments supplanted by legislatively imposed mandatory sentences that nullify their professional training and experience. Thus, we can expect to find pressures, similar to those found in teacher education, on the accreditation mechanisms in other professions. They too will be called on to provide solid evidence that their members are fully competent and qualified if they are to extricate themselves from intrusive and misplaced oversight by other bodies.

We should also expect to find that the assurance of quality in the other learned professions is, like teaching, beyond the capacity of accreditation itself and that it inevitably entails the mechanisms of licensure, certification, peer review, employment, and so forth. The decisions made about the granting of employment, the professional license, certificate, merit award, and honors should be based more on solid evidence of accomplishment than on conformity to standards, largely unvalidated, and established by mere consensus of the members of the profession.

Notes

1. Project 30 was a similar initiative that extended to all kinds of institutions of higher education, not just the research universities, and stressed depth in the liberal arts education of prospective teachers. The group continues as the Project 30 Alliance, with teams of education and liberal arts faculty from approximately thirty institutions.

2. See Murray (1996) for an account of the overall tentative nature of the knowledge base for teacher education, despite solid advances in some domains. See also Raths (1999) for some reasons that the current standards are merely hypotheses.

3. Note, for example, that the Council for Basic Education, the Fordham Foundation, and the American Federation of Teachers have not found consistency in the curriculum standards of the various states. See also Archbald (1998) for an account of these discrepancies. Along the same lines, the validation of the INTASC, NCATE, and NBPTS standards is only now beginning as part of the National Partnership for Excellence and Accountability in Teaching Office of Educational Research and Improvement contract. In the preliminary findings, NCATE graduates, for example, have generally not shown a superiority over non-NCATE graduates (Ballou and M.

Podgursky, 1999). Gitomer, Latham, and Ziomek (1999), however, found that overall, graduates of NCATE-accredited schools, despite their lower SAT or ACT scores, did have slightly higher pass rates on state licensure examinations in their subjects than graduates of non-NCATE schools, although there is considerable variability in the data among the various teaching fields and the location of the academic major. Wenglinsky (2000) analyzed data from forty thousand prospective teachers in 152 programs and found only five factors that led to higher scores on the licensure test. Accreditation was not one of them.

4. The NBPTS has released data that indicate that a sample of thirty-one of its certified teachers, in contrast to a sample of thirty-four it did not certify, scored higher in eleven of thirteen areas of teaching expertise that were drawn from the research literature on teaching effectiveness (*Education Week*, 2000).

5. Apart from the sad fact that a majority of graduates of Massachusetts colleges were unable to pass the state's new license test was the equally unsettling fact that apparently so few institutions had better evidence of their graduates' worth with which to rebut the test results, despite their legitimate protestations of the new test's weaknesses. Thus, the debate in Massachusetts and elsewhere was determined and shaped, in the absence of more compelling evidence, by the test results, the only empirical evidence available. A new accreditation system would provide compelling evidence because the accreditation decision would be based on it (Haney and others, 1999).

6. For example: Are the grades the faculty give consistent with other known measures of accomplishment? Do they measure only what they are supposed to measure? Do they predict later accomplishment and success? Are the differences between them real. Is there grade inflation? Are they the appropriate basis for high-stakes decisions?

7. Consider, for example, the following test of a student's ability to form a category: "Delete the element that doesn't belong with the others: violin, drum, guitar, cello." *Drum* is the correct choice, of course, but a student familiar with symphony orchestras might delete *guitar,* and a student unfamiliar with musical instruments might delete *cello* on the view that the other three were musical instruments and *cello* was simply unknown. In each case, there would be equivalent mental functioning with respect to the underlying skill of the formation of a class or category, yet in only one case would it have been recognized. In sum, we would be misled in our inference of the abilities of those who deleted *guitar* or *cello.*

8. See, for example, Darling-Hammond (2000).

References

Archbald, D. (1998). "The Reviews of State Content Standards in English Language Arts and Mathematics: A Summary and Review of Their Methods And Findings and Implications for Future Standards Development." Unpublished report for the National Education Goals Panel, 1998.

Ballou, D., and Podgursky, M. "Teacher Training and Licensure: A Layman's Guide." In M. Kanstoroom and C. Finn (eds.), *Better Teachers, Better Schools.* Washington, D.C.: Thomas Fordham Foundation, 1999.

Blits, J. *The American University: Problems, Prospects and Trends.* Buffalo, N.Y.: Prometheus Books, 1985.

Carnegie Forum on Education and the Economy. *A Nation Prepared: Teachers for the Twenty-First Century.* Washington, D.C.: Carnegie Forum, 1996.

Conant, J. B. *Education of American Teachers*. New York: McGraw-Hill, 1963.

Darling-Hammond, L. (ed.). *Studies of Excellence in Teacher Education*. Washington, D.C.: American Association of Colleges for Teacher Education Publications, 2000.

Dill, D., Massy, W., Williams, P., and Cook, C. "Accreditation and Academic Quality Assurance: Can We Get There from Here?" *Change Magazine*, Sept.–Oct. 1996, pp. 17–24.

Education Week, Oct. 25, 2000, p. 1.

Ferguson, R. "Paying for Public Education: New Evidence of How and Why Money Matters." *Harvard Journal on Legislation*, 1991, 465–498.

Gitomer, D., Latham, A., and Ziomek, R. *The Academic Quality of Prospective Teachers: The Impact of Admissions and Licensure Testing*. 1999.

Graham, P., Lyman, R., and Trow, M. *Accountability of Colleges and Universities: An Essay*. New York: Columbia University Press, 1995.

Haney, W., and others. "Less Truth Than Error? An Independent Study of the Massachusetts Teacher Tests." *Education Policy Analysis Archive*. [www.olam.ed.asu.edu/epaa/v7n4/]. 1999.

Judge, H., Lemosse, M., Paine, M., and Sedlak, M. *The University and the Teachers*. Oxford Studies in Comparative Education 4 (1–2). Wallingsford, Oxfordshire, United Kingdom: Triangle Books, 1994.

Koerner, J. D. *The Miseducation of American Teachers*. Boston: Houghton Mifflin, 1963.

Meier, D. *Will Standards Save Public Education?* Boston: Beacon Press, 2000.

Mitchell, R., and Barth, P. "How Teacher Licensing Tests Fall Short." *Thinking K-16*, 1999, 3(1).

Murray, F. "Teaching Strategies and Conservation Training." In A. M. Lesgold, J. W. Pellegrino, S. Fokkema, and R. Glaser (eds.), *Cognitive Psychology and Instruction*. New York: Plenum, 1978.

Murray, F. "The Conversion of Truth into Necessity." In W. Overton (ed.), *Reasoning, Necessity and Logic: Developmental Perspectives*. Hillsdale, N. J.: Erlbaum, 1990.

Murray, F. "Restructuring and Constructivism: The Development of American Educational Reform." In H. Beilin and P. Pufall (eds.), *Piaget's Theory: Prospects and Possibilities*. Hillsdale, N.J.: Erlbaum, 1992.

Murray, F. (ed.). *The Teacher Educator's Handbook: Building a Knowledge Base for the Preparation of Teachers*. San Francisco: Jossey-Bass, 1996.

National Commission on Excellence in Education. *A Nation at Risk*. Washington, D.C.: U.S. Government Printing Office, 1983.

National Commission on Teaching and America's Future. *What Matters Most: Teaching for America's Future*. New York: National Commission on Teaching and America's Future, 1996.

Ohanian, S. *One Size Fits Few: The Folly of Educational Standards*. New York: Heinemann, 1999.

Ohanian, S. "Goals 200: What's in a Name?" *Phi Delta Kappan*, Jan. 2000, pp. 345–355.

Raths, J. "A Consumer's Guide to Teacher Standards." *Kappan*, 1999, 81(3).

Sanders, W., and Rivers, J. *Cumulative and Residual Effects of Teachers on Future Student Academic Achievement*. Knoxville: University of Tennessee Value-Added Research and Development Center, 1996.

Smith, L. *Necessary Knowledge: Piagetian Perspectives on Constructivism*. Hillsdale, N.J.: Erlbaum. 1993.

Teacher Education Accreditation Council. *Prospectus*. Washington, D.C.: Teacher Education Accreditation Council, 1999.

Trow, M. "On the Accountability of Higher Education in the United States." In W. Bowen and H. Shapiro (eds.), *Universities and Their Leadership*. Princeton, N.J.: Princeton University Press, 1998.

Wenglinsky, H. *Teaching Teachers: Different Settings, Different Results*. Princeton, N.J.: Policy Information Center, Educational Testing Service, 2000. (ETS)

Wright, S., Horn, S., and Sanders, W. "Teacher and Classroom Context Effects on Student Achievement: Implications for Teacher Evaluation." *Journal of Personnel Evaluation in Education,* 1997, 57–67.

FRANK BRUSH MURRAY is H. Rodney Sharp Professor in the School of Education and Department of Psychology at the University of Delaware and Director of the Center for Educational Leadership and Policy. He is also president of the Teacher Education Accreditation Council in Washington, D.C.

5

*Accreditation standards change in response
to a variety of external and internal factors
but invariably come to reflect the expectations
of the members of the accrediting body.*

How Frequently Should Accreditation Standards Change?

Cynthia A. Davenport

Major standards revisions are a lot of hard work, often taking several years to complete. Reaching consensus always involves many, many drafts and many hearings. At the start of one comprehensive revision, I had to make a choice between going for a root canal procedure and going to the standards revision meeting. I chose the root canal. It was much faster and less painful!

Whether you are on the doing end or the receiving end, it would be unusual to look forward to a revision of accreditation standards. Program directors, deans, institutional administrators, and those who are affiliated in some way with an accrediting body can certainly present a case either for or against making changes in accreditation standards. Standards must change often enough to ensure that students receive the education they want and pay for. Students have the right to expect to receive an education that has adequately prepared them to enter into their intended field of work or practice, especially if they have studied in a professional field. Employers should be able to rely on being able to hire students who are ready, or nearly ready, to be productive employees. However, education benefits from continuity, and institutions and programs have the right to expect a certain amount of stability. They need to be confident that changes in the standards will not be arbitrary or capricious. They need to know that the standards are created and changed based on consensus developed by review of widespread input from broad communities of interest.

Link Between Standards and Outcomes

Prior to the 1980s, accreditation standards focused largely on processes, procedures, and the inputs that were supposed to result in educated, well-prepared students. When the conversation within higher education began to focus on

NEW DIRECTIONS FOR HIGHER EDUCATION, no. 113, Spring 2001 © Jossey-Bass, A Publishing Unit of John Wiley & Sons, Inc.

results, outputs, and outcomes, many accrediting bodies, especially in the specialized and professional fields, began to incorporate outcomes into their accreditation standards and reviews more consciously. The accreditation community, both institutional and specialized, has moved a long way from the stereotype of bean counters who want only to count the number of books in the library. In fact, for an accreditor to be recognized by the U.S. secretary of education, the agency must have standards in ten areas that are "sufficiently rigorous to ensure that the agency is a reliable authority regarding the quality of the education or training provided by the institutions or programs it accredits" (*Federal Register,* 1999, p. 56620). One of those ten standards is: "Success with respect to student achievement in relation to the institution's mission" (*Federal Register,* 1999, p. 56620). Regional and national institutional accreditors have perhaps found this Department of Education mandate somewhat more challenging than have specialized accreditors. Results and outcomes have always been important to educators and accreditors who work within the framework of a specific discipline or field, especially when the field has its own individually focused certifying, licensing, or other such examination to validate the readiness of graduates for entry into practice. In spite of this history, many programs and institutions are still learning better ways of assessing the result of the education they provide to students.

Beginning in the 1980s, the staff of many specialized accrediting agencies began working with their decision-making bodies to incorporate a more specific emphasis on outcomes into the accreditation process. The accrediting agency's decision-making body (often called a commission, council, or governing board), not staff, sets standards, adopts policies and procedures, and takes action on accreditation reviews. The accrediting agency's staff, however, often functions as the glue that holds day-to-day operations together. It is members of the staff who implement the actions and decisions made by the commission or council. In general, it was necessary for staff to help the governing body understand that it would not be unduly burdensome to ask the accredited program or school to provide evidence of the results achieved by the education provided to students. Similarly, the accredited programs or schools needed to be convinced that they would be able to meet such a requirement when it was incorporated into the accreditation standards. Accrediting agencies needed to be responsive to the many concerns expressed by their communities of interest. Some accreditors addressed the apprehension of their educational constituencies by adopting a new standard that required the programs to provide evidence of student achievement (learning outcomes) while also setting a later-than-usual implementation date (the date by which programs must demonstrate compliance with the standard). Typically two or three years were allotted (rather than the more typical twelve months) to give programs sufficient time to meet the new standard. During that same time, accreditors developed resource materials to assist programs in creating assessment plans that were linked to the goals and objectives of the program within the broader context of the institution.

In general, accrediting bodies have used one of two main methods to incorporate outcomes assessment into their standards. The earliest groups added a new standard that required the accredited program to develop and implement a cyclical plan for ongoing assessment using multiple measures. "Ongoing" and "multiple measures" are key phrases here, as is the requirement that the plan be based on the program's own goals and objectives. The other main approach requires a comprehensive revision of the accreditation standards. During the revision process, some accrediting bodies have chosen to rewrite the standards with a competency-based focus, speaking about what students will "learn to do" as a result of the educational program. However, assessing the effectiveness of competency-based education should also take place within the context of the program's own goals and objectives, involve multiple measures, and include a cyclical plan that uses the assessment results to improve the overall quality of the program.

As has been true of other trends in education, the pendulum related to reliance on educational outcomes has now swung toward the other end of the continuum. Those who once argued against the use of outcome measures now assert that such measures should take precedence over all others. Accreditors, faced with forces that are pushing them toward further (or even sole) reliance on outcomes, assert that it would not be in the best interest of the students to focus only on results. It would not be in the best interest of students to ignore the selected processes (or inputs) that allow accrediting agencies to speak about the "likely assurance" that an accredited program or institution will continue to offer quality education. The U.S. Department of Education agrees that outcomes alone are not sufficient indicators of quality. The *Federal Register's* preamble to the 1999 revised regulations for recognition of accrediting agencies included the following comment:

> Demonstrating success with respect to student achievement is certainly necessary to establishing the adequacy of an agency's standards. *By itself, however, such a demonstration is by no means sufficient to ensure the adequacy of those standards* [emphasis added] [U.S. Department of Education, 1999, p. 56615].

Standards are consensus documents. Standards can be effective only if they emerge from the collective wisdom of the broad-based constituencies affected by the accreditation process. For example, the communities of interest that might typically have input into the revision of nurse anesthesia accreditation standards include the Council on Public Interest in Anesthesia, the Council on Certification of Nurse Anesthetists, the Council on Recertification of Nurse Anesthetists, the board of directors of the American Association of Nurse Anesthetists, the U.S. Department of Education's Division of Accreditation and State Liaison, related professional associations, state boards of nursing, nurse anesthesia educational programs, chief executive officers of institutions that conduct a nurse anesthesia educational program, and any other groups or agencies deemed appropriate (typically because of specific concerns or interests) (Council on Accreditation of Nurse Anesthesia Educational Programs, 1996).

The American Council on Pharmaceutical Education also circulates draft revised standards to a broad-based community of interest. It routinely includes the following constituencies: the dean of colleges and schools of pharmacy having accredited programs and their respective institutional administrative officers, faculties, and students; the chief executive officer of state boards of pharmacy for consideration by their respective boards; the governing boards of the American Association of Colleges of Pharmacy, American Pharmaceutical Association, National Association of Boards of Pharmacy, American Council on Education, and other professional organizations and societies significantly affected by the accreditation process. Draft documents are circulated to these groups for further dissemination among their members for comment. Copies are made available to the public on request, and open hearings are held prior to any final revision or action (American Council on Pharmaceutical Education, 2000).

Achieving consensus within such a wide range of groups can seem monumental, but the staff and governing bodies of accrediting agencies know that without consensus, the standards will not be successful. Accreditation occurs by invitation of those accredited; it is not imposed by the accreditor. Thus, in the face of often conflicting pressures, accreditors must and do continue to work with their communities of interest to find the appropriate balance between process and outcomes and for other equally important aspects of the standards (choices relating to curriculum or protection of students in laboratory settings, for example).

Code of Good Practice of the Association of Specialized and Professional Accreditors

In 1995, the members of the Association of Specialized and Professional Accreditors (ASPA) unanimously adopted a seven-point *Code of Good Practice* that remains the cornerstone for its membership.[1] An accrediting organization holding membership in ASPA "focuses accreditation reviews on the development of knowledge and competence," according to the fifth item of the ASPA *Code*. The following four subpoints of the fifth item explain a member accreditor's duties (ASPA, 1995, p. 2):

- Concentrates on results in light of specific institutional and programmatic missions, goals, objectives, and contexts
- Deals comprehensively with relationships and interdependencies among purposes, aspirations, curricula, operations, resources, and results
- Considers techniques, methods, and resources primarily in light of results achieved and functions fulfilled rather than the reverse

- Has standards and review procedures that provide room for experimentation, encourage responsible innovation, and promote thoughtful evolution

The ASPA *Code* reflects the importance of results and outcomes but retains sufficient focus on the processes and procedures to allow accreditors to fulfill their public responsibilities and provide certain assurances to prospective students and their parents. Although a program or school meets accreditation standards and has demonstrated certain outcomes at the time of an on-site review, accreditors also look to see what processes or procedures were in place to help the school achieve its results. Including structure, organization, or process in the review allows the accreditor to speak to the likelihood of continued compliance with the standards. Accreditors must be reasonably certain that a program, school, or institution will continue to meet the accreditation standards during the period between on-site reviews. Not only do prospective students and their parents expect this, but the U.S. Department of Education requires it of all of its recognized accreditors.

U.S. Department of Education Requirements

All accrediting agencies (national, regional, and specialized) recognized by the U.S. Department of Education must meet the following requirements in section 602.21 (Review of Standards) related to review of their accreditation standards:[2]

(a) The agency must maintain a systematic program of review that demonstrates that its standards are adequate to evaluate the quality of the education or training provided by the institutions and programs it accredits and relevant to the educational or training needs of students.

(b) The agency determines the specific procedures it follows in evaluating its standards, but the agency must ensure that its program of review—

(1) Is comprehensive;

(2) Occurs at regular, yet reasonable, intervals or on an ongoing basis;

(3) Examines each of the agency's standards and the standards as a whole; and

(4) Involves all of the agency's relevant constituencies in the review and affords them a meaningful opportunity to provide input into the review.

(c) If the agency determines, at any point during its systematic program of review, that it needs to make changes to its standards, the agency must initiate action within 12 months to make the changes and must complete that action within a reasonable period of time. Before finalizing any changes to its standards, the agency must—

(1) Provide notice to all of the agency's relevant constituencies, and other parties who have made their interest known to the agency, of the changes the agency proposes to make;

(2) Give the constituencies and other interested parties adequate opportunity to comment on the proposed changes; and

(3) Take into account any comments on the proposed changes submitted timely by the relevant constituencies and by other interested parties [*Federal Register,* 1999, p. 56621].

The required elements are reflected in various ways in the written policies or procedures of department-recognized accrediting agencies. The accreditation community is very pleased that the July 1, 2000, regulations no longer use the terms "validity and reliability" and appreciates the department's awareness of the burden that the use of that statistical language imposed. Still, the accreditors are very much aware that the department continues to require them to conduct comprehensive, ongoing assessment of the effectiveness of the accreditation standards and, when change is needed, to initiate it promptly. Because the requirement remains, accreditors will continue to follow the assessment schedules or formulas reflected in their written validity and reliability policy statements. The Commission on Dental Accreditation (CDA) and the Joint Review Committee on Education in Radiologic Technology (JRCERT) have written policy that includes an assessment formula. The formula requires that the standards be assessed when they have been in place for an amount of time equal to the length of the educational program plus three years. This means that standards for a twelve-month educational program would be assessed after they had been in place for four years, while the standards for a four-year educational program would be assessed after they had been in place for seven years. In addition, the CDA and JRCERT policies mandate review after the standards have been in place for five years to determine if revision is needed. Although the regulatory language changed in July 2000, accreditors know that it is their responsibility to examine their standards (individually and as a whole), consult with their communities of interest, and make determinations about the appropriateness of change.

In addition to the requirements cited, the U.S. Department of Education specifies a minimum amount of time within which an accredited program or institution must "take appropriate action to bring itself into compliance with the agency's standards" (*Federal Register,* 2000, p. 56620, sec. 602.20). The amount of time ranges from twelve to twenty-four months, depending on the length of the educational program. These regulations also state: "If the institution or program does not bring itself into compliance within the specified period, the agency must take immediate adverse action unless the agency, for good cause, extends the period for achieving compliance" (p. 56621).

This federal requirement has caused some accreditors to look at their standards from a somewhat different perspective. One accreditor told me that the twelve-month rule forced that commission to take a hard look at the standards. Some were eliminated because they were not viewed as sufficiently important to justify removing a program's accreditation status if the program were still out of compliance by the due date set in the accreditation visit and review.

Recognition Process of the Council for Higher Education Accreditation

Since 1975, there has also been a nongovernmental process for recognition of specialized, regional, and national institutional accrediting organizations. Reviews were conducted from 1975 to 1993 by the Council on Postsecondary Accreditation and from 1994 to 1996 by the Commission on Recognition of Postsecondary Accreditation (CORPA). The Council for Higher Education Accreditation (CHEA) assumed CORPA's review responsibilities when it was formed in 1996 but developed a new approach to recognition that it intends to be more results centered. This new approach to recognition is still being implemented. The first wave of eligibility reviews was conducted in 1999, and CHEA's Committee on Recognition conducted the first recognition reviews during 2000, with anticipated action by the CHEA board in early 2001.

CHEA (1998) states that its recognition of accrediting organizations has three basic purposes:

TO ADVANCE ACADEMIC QUALITY. To confirm that accrediting organizations have standards that advance academic quality in higher education; that those standards emphasize student achievement and high expectations of teaching and learning, research, and service; and that those standards are developed within the framework of institutional mission.

TO DEMONSTRATE ACCOUNTABILITY. To confirm that accrediting organizations have standards that ensure accountability through consistent, clear, and coherent communication to the public and the higher education community about the results of educational efforts. Accountability also includes a commitment by the accrediting organization to involve the public in accreditation decision-making.

TO ENCOURAGE PURPOSEFUL CHANGE AND NEEDED IMPROVEMENT. To confirm that accrediting organizations have standards that encourage institutions to plan, where needed, for purposeful change and improvement; to develop and sustain activities that anticipate and address needed change; to stress student achievement; and to ensure long-range institutional viability [Sec. II, Item 5, p. 3].

CHEA has five recognition standards.[3] Although the structure and emphasis of its requirements differ greatly from those of the U.S. Department of Education, CHEA (1998) too requires public involvement in the development of the accreditation standards and expects recognized accreditors to have "appropriate processes to respond to legitimate public concerns and complaints" (Sec. III, Item 11B, pp. 4–5).

Although CHEA does not speak specifically to processes that accreditors use to revise standards, it is likely that accreditors will follow the framework developed to meet the Department of Education requirements. Required or not, accreditors believe it is good practice to provide notice of proposed changes, review the comments received from many audiences, and balance them with the many other intangible factors that surround revisions of the standards. But after all the input has been received and the study is completed, the decision of whether to revise one, all, or none of the standards is a judgment based on the collective wisdom of the accreditation decision makers. Whether there are many changes or none, the buck stops with the final action of the accrediting body. The revised standards are adopted by the accrediting body and implemented by the accredited programs. Then, all too soon it often seems, the process of review and revision may begin again.

By show of hands at a September 2000 meeting of the Chicago Area Accreditors, nearly everyone in the room indicated that they maintained an accreditation standards revision folder. Over time, this folder is filled with standards received from accreditation colleagues, comments, criticisms, interesting ideas, creative examples, notes on things to try or things to avoid, and assorted other standards-related items. No matter how recently a revision was completed, all accreditors know that another revision is waiting just over the horizon, so they file helpful tips and ideas with the nonurgent comments to "be addressed next time." Some accreditors (Marriage and Family Therapy, for example) report yearly on the state of the accreditation standards and interpretations to the commission, in addition to keeping comments and issues on file for consideration during the next revision (Commission on Accreditation for Marriage and Family Therapy Education, 1997).

Survey of Specialized Accreditors

In August 2000, I conducted an informal survey of the specialized accreditor members of ASPA and reviewed participants' written policy and procedures statements governing revision of accreditation standards. The survey and written statements provided a broader perspective to the question of when and how often accreditation standards change. (Although many of the observations may apply to regional or national institutional accreditors, those groups were not included in the survey. For this reason, the following remarks are limited to specialized and professional accreditors.)

In general, the survey results show that specialized and professional accreditors believe standards must change often enough to keep up with changes in the profession or field but not so often as to be burdensome to the accredited programs or schools. U.S. Department of Education–recognized accreditors are reluctant to make significant changes too often; frequent changes would make it more difficult for them to assess the adequacy and relevance (formerly validity and reliability) of their standards and review process. Roughly two-thirds of the ASPA member accreditors are recognized by the U.S. Secretary of Education.[4]

About two-thirds of the ASPA-member accreditors are recognized by CHEA, but these are not necessarily the same two-thirds recognized by the U.S. Department of Education.[5] The first wave of accreditors was reviewed by CHEA for recognition in the fall of 2000. Because the CHEA process is in its early stages, accreditors have no firsthand experience with what CHEA may expect when it comes to revision of the standards. Thus, very few aspects of the survey directly relate to the CHEA recognition process. The biggest concern for accreditors at this point is what they will do if it turns out that some elements of the CHEA and U.S. Department of Education requirements conflict with each other. If that were to happen, it could cause problems not only for the accreditors but also for their accredited programs or schools. Clearly, the environment in which any change in standards must take place is complex.

Revisions Governed by Written Policies or Procedures. Since 1975, accrediting bodies have adopted written policies that speak to the frequency with which their standards are reviewed and the processes used for the review. Fourteen survey respondents said that their standards revision was triggered by the passage of time. Review of written policy statements revealed that the amount of time between revisions varied from ongoing to ten years, with five years being the most typical amount of time between reviews. Two agencies, Chiropractic (Council on Chiropractic Education, 2000) and American Veterinary Medical Association, use a "continuous" plan of review, with roughly one-fourth of the standards being reviewed during each year of a four-year cycle and then the standards as a whole being reviewed during the fifth year. When revisions are triggered by time, most accreditors conduct a study to determine whether the current standards continue to serve or whether revision is warranted.

Results of Standards Review and Scope of Revision. Even if not specifically stated in written policy, accreditors typically base the scope of any subsequent revision on the results of their assessment of the need for revision. For example, the Commission on Dental Accreditation (American Dental Association, 2000) cites four possible results of an assessment review:

- Authorization of a comprehensive revision of the standards
- Revision of specific sections of the standards
- Refinement/clarification of portions of the standards
- No changes in the standards but use of this assessment during the next revision [p. 54].

Essentially the same options are written into policy adopted by the Joint Review Committee on Education in Radiologic Technology (1997), and the American Veterinary Medical Association (2000) states that as a result of its process of continuous review, "standards may be revised or refined for clarification, undergo no change, be dropped, or be subjected to comprehensive revision resulting in a more effective means of assessing the veterinary medical programs" (p. 12).

Accreditors classify revision of standards as being comprehensive, substantive, or editorial or nonsubstantive). A comprehensive revision would include significant changes to many or all standards or perhaps a new approach or significant shift in emphasis. A change to competency-based standards, for example, is a comprehensive standards revision. A substantive revision encompasses important changes to one or more standards— for example, addition of a new standard requiring accredited programs to provide evidence of outcomes or student achievement. Editorial or nonsubstantive revisions, as the name suggests, are noncontroversial small adjustments intended to clarify or improve the standards. The scope of these three types of revisions is quite different, and all have an important place in the accreditation world.

Not every change to the standards is comprehensive. In fact, some accreditors favor the "earthquake method" (frequent small tremors to prevent a major shake). When asked what issues would influence the decision to initiate a comprehensive revision to accreditation standards, the most frequent answer was major changes in the profession or field, although changes in geographic or academic scope and numerous requests from constituents were also listed.

Less significant changes in the profession, distance education or changes in technology, changes in views about good accreditation practice, changes in governmental or nongovernmental recognition requirements, and efforts to improve the quality and effectiveness of accreditation and the profession were listed as changes that would typically result in substantive but not necessarily comprehensive changes to the standards. One respondent commented that balance is achieved by weighing "seriousness" with frequency, adding, "Making minor adjustments as you go along prevents having to do a major revision too often." Another respondent says her agency may "refine" the standards between five-year reviews based on experience. Although "refinement" is more than tinkering and less than a comprehensive review from the accreditor's perspective, the respondent admits that institutions may not view it as being much different.

Costs Associated with Changes in Standards. There are always costs associated with new standards. ASPA chair David J. Werner (March 28, 1999 personal communication), chancellor of Southern Illinois University in Edwardsville, says that the biggest cost of accreditation is that of complying with the accreditation standards. At the spring 1999 ASPA meeting, Werner used an informal skit, "The Devil Made Me Do It," to generate a lively discussion of perceptions versus realities and uses or misuses of accreditation standards. The skit used humor to illustrate a program director who was overstating the burden of preparing for an accreditation review and blatantly misusing accreditation standards in an attempt to leverage increased resources from higher-level institutional administrators. Werner says that institutional administrators need to accept the responsibility for becoming informed about the standards for the specialized and professional programs offered at their institution. This would limit the ability of program directors, deans, and other institutional personnel to use the accreditation standards to leverage resources that the program or school might like to have but are in no way mandated by the standards. Accreditors may know that this leveraging happens within institutions, but in the absence of high-level administrators who are better informed, accreditors have limited ability to defend themselves against these often unfair charges. For this reason, ASPA member accreditors continue to seek ways to communicate more directly and effectively with institutional presidents and provosts.

Accrediting agencies have become increasingly sensitive to costs that extend beyond those to the agency. They have reexamined both real and perceived costs to their members and consider both as they assess the frequency of revising their standards. Answers in the survey were about equally divided between yes and no to the survey question asking whether cost to the program or institution was factored into the decision. The split response may be explained by a respondent who noted, "Cost of specific changes is a factor, but not a factor in the decision to investigate the need for change," and another wrote, "Cost to programs is a consideration in every decision."

In addition, review of written statements revealed two accreditors whose policies require that cost be factored into the revision process. One of six conditions to be met for submitting a proposal for substantive change to the National Council for Accreditation of Teacher Education (NCATE) standards states, "The estimated cost to NCATE-accredited institutions of implementing the changes must be included" (2000, p. 22). Similarly, the Council for Accreditation of Counseling and Related Educational Programs (CACREP) has a policy that states, "Those making standards proposals must be sensitive to the needs that program staff will have in attempting to meet any new requirement. . . . The proposal shall illustrate how the new statements will be applied in practice including the implications for cost to CACREP and/or institutions in the application of these statements as standards to be met for accreditation" (2000a, p. 26).

Anticipation of lower costs has led to coordinating the on-site reviews of several agencies. Although it is not clear that coordinated site visit reviews save time or money, there are other positive reasons for two or more accrediting bodies to work cooperatively with a requesting institution to coordinate reviews of programs, perhaps with a regional or other institutional review. At the request of the institution, the Joint Review Committee on Education in Radiologic Technology (1997) will rely on the regional accreditor to review certain institutional components that it has used to review. CACREP (2000b) has adjusted its review cycle to coincide with the eight-year cycle used by the Council on Rehabilitation Education (CORE). CACREP and CORE (2000) have developed a joint self-study process for use when an institution sponsors programs in both fields and wishes to have them reviewed at the same time. Similar activities are occurring in other fields. The four arts accrediting agencies (Art and Design, Dance, Music, and Theatre) have a long history of working cooperatively with institutional accreditors to coordinate many reviews of free-standing single-purpose institutions (National Association of Schools of Art and Design, National Association of Schools of Dance, National Association of Schools of Music, National Association of Schools of Theatre, 1999). Nursing and nurse anesthesia have also conducted cooperative reviews at the request of the sponsoring institution, as have many other accreditors. For some cooperative efforts, results are still coming in. For others, the goodwill generated by responsiveness to institutional requests and concerns seems to offset any additional burdens imposed. The review may not be less work or cost less, but the involved parties "feel better" about it, and in the end, wise accreditors know that how the programs or schools feel about a review—or about the standards—may be what matters most.

Circulating Proposed Changes. Accreditation standards, even for the licensed professions where accreditation may be more mandatory than voluntary, are consensus documents. Accreditors seek input from broad-based communities and interested parties to develop standards that most, if not all, agree will result in competent, well-educated graduates. As executive director of ASPA, I often receive calls from individuals representing unaccredited areas of study. They call to ask me how they can start an accreditation program for their field. First, I ask what they have done to explore whether any existing processes would meet their needs. Then I ask them to tell me why they want to go to the considerable effort to start and run a good accreditation program. Often they say they want to be an accreditor so they can "control the standards." That response tells me that the caller knows very little about how accreditation standards are developed, and I plunge into the speech that begins, "In order to be effective, standards must reflect the consensus of those to whom they will be applied." Probably any reputable accreditor could do that speech in unison with me, and what we would be saying is true. The standard revision process must build consensus, or there will be a huge price to pay and ultimately the standards will not be successful.

Without fail, accreditors provide significant opportunities for written or oral (or both) comments on the proposed draft standards as part of the consensus-building process. All department-recognized accreditors are required to circulate proposed revisions in the standards to "all of the agency's relevant constituencies, and other parties who have made their interest known to the agency," giving the constituencies and other interested parties "adequate opportunity" to comment on the proposed changes (Federal Register,

1999, p. 56621). According to CHEA Recognition Standard 11D (1998), CHEA-recognized accreditors must involve "higher education professionals and the public in decision-making about accreditation policies and procedures" (p. 7).

Accreditors seek comment because to do so is consistent with good accreditation practice. However, not all accreditors routinely include as part of their community of interest an institutional administrator who is at a level higher than that of the program director or dean. Respondents to the survey were split on this question, with six saying no, eight saying yes, and one saying both yes and no because a proposed revision goes to a high-level institutional administrator in some settings but not others. By allowing the program director or dean to manage the standards review process within his or her own institution, accreditors leave themselves vulnerable to comments from institutional presidents or provosts who claim (accurately in some cases) that they have never seen or had a chance to comment on proposed standards for professional programs.

Adopting Standards. For comprehensive reviews and revisions, most accrediting bodies form a standards revision committee to oversee the process. The committee typically includes members from the varied communities affected by the standards. The committee may receive a draft revised document from some source (the source can vary) or develop a draft based on the issues that led to the decision to initiate a revision. When the drafts have been developed and circulated and the open hearings have been held and the many comments accepted or rejected, a final draft document is prepared. In most cases, that final draft is forwarded to the decision-making body for action. In some cases, the membership of the accrediting organization votes to adopt the standards. Many accrediting bodies are not structured as membership organizations. The four arts accrediting organizations and the International Association for Management Education are structured in this manner (International Association for Management Education, 1998). For them, those who must comply with the standards vote whether to impose them on themselves.

Implementation of Standards. When asked how much time is typically allowed before revised standards go into effect, responses varied from zero months to two years, depending on the degree and nature of the revision. For comprehensive revision of the standards, ten respondents reported that implementation dates are typically set twelve months from the date of adoption to give programs or schools time to comply. Three respondents typically set implementation dates more than twelve months after the date of adoption, while only two give less than twelve months for comprehensive revisions. Implementation dates for noncomprehensive revisions range from "immediate" to as long as twelve months, with somewhere between six and twelve months being most typical.

When comprehensive changes are made or during the period when new standards have been adopted but not yet implemented, several accrediting bodies reported that they allow programs or schools to select which version of the standards they wish to use for an upcoming review. NCATE states that it is making a transition from its old standards to its significantly changed standards based on performance data over a five-year period during which the standards may be refined. The accrediting bodies for acupuncture and for nurse anesthesia include an interesting element in their standards development process: "trial standards," when they seek feedback on any problems that programs or schools may experience as they come into compliance with the revisions.

Revision Response Time. The typical process followed for revising standards includes many steps that can take months or even a year or two. A new accrediting body, in the process of developing its first set of accreditation standards, held five regional hearings to receive comments. Those standards went through ten revisions, which resulted in reducing the number of standards from ten to four. Using a multistep process like this allows accreditors to generate consensus. The downside is the appearance that change in the world of accreditation takes forever. Some have asserted that accreditors use their established processes as a way to delay change, but far more often the process is used to protect, not prevent. Accreditors know that they must be able to respond quickly when urgent issues arise. Two survey participants, the Council on Accreditation of Nurse Anesthesia Educational Programs and the Commission on Accreditation for Marriage and Family Therapy Education, have written procedures that include a fast-track option. This option allows them to address changes necessitated by law or of such urgency that the normal process would not suffice.

Conclusion

Having reviewed more than twenty written policy and procedural statements, what are my conclusions about how often standards should be revised? Perhaps my short answer is the point at which I began: often enough to be responsive but not so often as to be burdensome or intrusive.

Those who believe that accreditation standards change too often should be reassured by the detailed consensus-building processes that accreditors use. Those who believe professional standards are self-serving should be reassured by the broad-based audiences routinely included in the revision process. Educators in accredited programs should be reassured by knowing that they will have a chance to comment on proposed changes and that the potential impact on the accredited programs or schools is always carefully assessed. Those who believe that accreditation standards do not change often enough may want to become more assertive in proposing changes and calling on other constituencies to support the proposed change. Similar comments received from varied sources quickly catch the attention of the accrediting organizations. When consensus exists, the standards will change.

As employers demand employees with new or different skills and as professions change, accreditation standards will be revised. As the requirements imposed on accreditors by the recognizing entities change, accreditation standards will be revised. As higher education changes, accreditation standards will be revised. If the environment surrounding the standards were to become stagnant, there might be no need for change, but I do not see that happening. For standards to remain the consensus documents I have asserted they are, they must change as the world they reflect changes. Change may indeed be inevitable, but the policies and procedures used by all accreditors, not just specialized and professional accreditors, provide a controlled framework within which the need for the change can be assessed and responsible revisions can occur.

Notes

1. The ASPA Code is available on the ASPA Web site: http://www.aspa-usa.org by clicking on the "Code of Ethics" button. The code is also located on pp. 3–4 of the 2000–2001 *ASPA Membership Directory*.
2. These regulations may be reviewed in the Federal Register Online via Government Printing Office Access (wais.access.gpo.gov) [DOCID:fr20oc99–29].
3. These materials are also available in the same section of the CHEA Web site: www.chea.org/About/Recognition/cfm.
4. Some accreditors are not eligible for U.S. Department of Education recognition. Following the 1992 amendments to the Higher Education Act, about a dozen accreditors were removed from the secretary's list in 1994 because they do not serve a gatekeeper role for Title IV or other federal monies.
5. Some accreditors are not eligible for CHEA recognition because the majority of their programs are not degree granting. An example would be when a large number of hospital-based programs are accredited.

References

American Council on Pharmaceutical Education. "Policy 6: Review, Revision, and Establishment of Standards." In *ACPE Accreditation Manual*. (9th ed.) Chicago: American Council on Pharmaceutical Education, Sept. 2000.
American Dental Association. Commission on Dental Accreditation. "1998 Policy: Development of Accreditation Standards" and "Policy on Assessing the Validity and Reliability of the Accreditation Standards." In *Evaluation Policies and Procedures*. Chicago: Commission on Dental Accreditation, July 2000.
American Veterinary Medical Association. "Development of Accreditation Standards." In *Accreditation Policies and Procedures of the AVMA Council on Education*. Schaumburg, Ill.: American Veterinary Medical Association Council on Education, Aug. 2000.
Association of Specialized and Professional Accreditors. "Code of Good Practice." In *2000–2001 ASPA Membership Directory*. [www.aspa-usa.org]. 1995.
Association of Specialized and Professional Accreditors. ASPA *Survey of Specialized and Professional Accreditors*. Chicago: Association of Specialized and Professional Accreditors, Aug. 2000.
Commission on Accreditation for Marriage and Family Therapy Education. "Standards Revision." In Commission on Accreditation for Marriage and Family Therapy, *Manual*

on Accreditation. Washington, D.C.: American Association for Marriage and Family Therapy, 1997.

Council for Accreditation of Counseling and Related Educational Programs. "Standards Revision: Policies and Procedures." In *CACREP Accreditation Manual.* Alexandria, Va.: Council for Accreditation of Counseling and Related Educational Programs, Aug. 2000a.

Council for Accreditation of Counseling and Related Educational Programs. "CACREP Changes Length of Accreditation Cycle." In *The CACREP Connection.* Alexandria, Va.: Council for Accreditation of Counseling and Related Educational Programs, Summer 2000b.

Council on Accreditation of Nurse Anesthesia Educational Programs. "Standards for Accreditation: Development, Adoption and Revision." In *1996 Accreditation Policies and Procedures.* Park Ridge, Ill.: Council on Accreditation of Nurse Anesthesia Educational Programs, 1996.

Council on Chiropractic Education. "Standards for Chiropractic Programs and Institutions, CCE Policy: BOD 22—CCE Bylaws and Standards Revision." In *CCE Policy Manual-BOD.* Scottsdale, Ariz.: Council on Chiropractic Education, May 2000.

Council for Higher Education Accreditation. "Recognition of Accrediting Organizations: Policy and Procedures." [http://www.chea.org.]. Sept. 28, 1998.

Council on Rehabilitation Education. "Accreditation Manual." [http://www.core-rehab .org/manual/manual.html]. Mar. 2000.

Federal Register. "Enforcement of Standards." Oct. 20, 2000, p. 56620, Section 602.20.

International Association for Management Education. "AACSB Accreditation Policies." In *Accreditation Policies and Procedures.* St. Louis, Mo.: International Association for Management Education, Jan. 1998.

Joint Review Committee on Education in Radiologic Technology. "Acceptable Evidence of Regional Accreditation Findings and Reports." *JRCERT Review,* Summer 1997, p. 7.

National Association of Schools of Art and Design, National Association of Schools of Dance, National Association of Schools of Music, National Association of Schools of Theatre. "Bylaws: Article IX: Accreditation Standards." In *1999–2000 Handbook.* Reston, Va.: National Association of Schools of Music, 1999.

National Council for Accreditation of Teacher Education. "Revisions to Standards and Indicators." In *Operating Procedures of the Unit Accreditation Board.* Washington, D.C.: National Council for Accreditation of Teacher Education, Mar. 2000.

U.S. Department of Commerce. In Federal Register. Rules and Regulations via GPO Access [on line]. Available: wais.access.gpo.gov. October 20, 1999. Volume 64(202), 56611–56626. [DOCID:fr20oc99_29].

Werner, D. J. "The Devil Made Me Do It." Skit presented at the Spring 1999 meeting of the Association of Specialized and Professional Accreditors, Arlington, Va., Mar. 29, 2000.

CYNTHIA A. DAVENPORT *is executive director of the Association of Specialized and Professional Accreditors.*

6

Electronic institutional portfolios can provide public access to information on student learning outcomes and institutional accountability.

Public Accountability and Reporting: What Should Be the Public Part of Accreditation?

Kathi A. Ketcheson

Advances in information technology have revolutionized the way colleges and universities collect, analyze, and report information about their activities. With the advent of Windows-based query languages, the Web, and other user-friendly computing tools, a wide variety of institutional data has become available to faculty, staff, students, and users outside the campus community. While access to information has many benefits, concerns over the responsible use and interpretation of data have increased. As one author has written, "Accessibility to data is not without its negative side, though, since there is no guarantee that all users, or suppliers either, will be informed or even well intentioned" (Sanford, 1995, p. 86).

Along with the ease in accessing information, expectations have risen that more data can and will be made available. Governing boards, accrediting agencies, and the public have increased their demands for accountability in higher education, placing pressure on colleges and universities to produce more data, often in new forms. Emphasis has been shifting from standard measures of performance, such as retention or graduation rates, to evidence of student learning. It is no longer sufficient for institutions to report data without also documenting outcomes and improvement.

What should be the public part of accreditation? How can institutions know how much and which data are of interest to external constituents? What are some of the issues surrounding the public communication of institutional data? How are institutions answering these questions, and how do their efforts relate to the processes of quality assurance and improvement that traditionally have been the goals of institutional accreditation?

NEW DIRECTIONS FOR HIGHER EDUCATION, no. 113, Spring 2001 © Jossey-Bass, A Publishing Unit of John Wiley & Sons, Inc. 83

The Use of Electronic Institutional Portfolios in Accreditation

In response to new demands in accreditation, many institutions are developing Web applications for documenting and reporting their activities. A renewed emphasis on student learning as a measure of institutional performance "enables institutions to focus their goals and improve their teaching and learning" (Morse and Santiago, 2000, p. 32). Electronic media, such as the Web, allow institutions to gather evidence of teaching and learning outcomes and other measures of performance in one virtual place, accessible to multiple publics in a dynamic environment. Contrasted with printed self-study reports, electronic portfolio sites allow information for accreditation and other purposes to be presented through a variety of media, including text, audio, video, and graphics. Web sites allow for layering of information through virtual links that allow users to develop a multidimensional view of the institution's activities.

The Urban Universities Portfolio Project. As a new direction in institutional assessment, accountability, and accreditation, the Urban Universities Portfolio Project (UUPP) is profiled in this chapter. The UUPP is a three-year project that began in 1998 and is funded by the Pew Charitable Trusts and sponsored by the American Association for Higher Education. Six urban institutions participated: California State University, Sacramento (CSUS); Georgia State University; Indiana University-Purdue University, Indianapolis (IUPUI); Portland State University (PSU); the University of Illinois at Chicago; and the University of Massachusetts at Boston. Emerging from national discussions on the reform of self-study practices in accreditation, the project sought to design a new medium for communicating quality assurance and institutional improvement information to the public. During its implementation, the project addressed many of the issues surrounding the public nature of accountability and accreditation information.

A portfolio is a folder, real or virtual, that contains information about a particular topic. Institutional portfolios contain examples of the institution's activities, programs, and initiatives, each expressing an element of reflection and self-assessment. Through its portfolio, an institution documents how it is achieving its stated mission by examples that speak to the interests of various audiences. A portfolio is not intended to showcase everything the institution is doing, but to feature examples of work that can be used to document improvement and accountability.

Susan Kahn (2000), national project director for the UUPP, described an electronic institutional portfolio as "a focused selection of authentic work, data, and reflection intended to demonstrate accountability and serve as a system for monitoring performance." It focuses on assessment, accountability, and improvement and is intended to present explicit evidence of the outcomes and effectiveness of urban public higher education to targeted audiences. In the UUPP portfolios, this evidence was linked directly to mission and its public communication and contrasted with traditional measures of performance, which tend to obscure mission differences and the complex nature of student enrollment patterns across institutions.

One of the aims of the project was to augment the self-study process through the use of Web-based institutional portfolios. Self-study documents typically are produced once every ten years, with a shorter update five years into the cycle; electronic institutional portfolios provide a more versatile, flexible, and continuous medium for communicating institutional work. In contrast to the weighty narratives that may characterize printed self-study reports, electronic portfolios can be updated frequently and adapted to changing circumstances. Effectiveness in meeting the institution's goals and accrediting standards can be documented in an interactive environment that allows users to experience the institution as well as read about it. To respond to an individual user's needs, printed copies of the portfolio can be made available as a companion to the electronic version.

Not all UUPP participants planned to use their portfolios as replacements for the traditional self-study report. CSUS and IUPUI had this as a primary objective, and PSU considered it a future goal. Others focused more explicitly on internal assessment or strategic planning efforts, specifying their internal campus communities as primary audiences for the portfolios. Whether intended for internal or external audiences, the UUPP portfolios highlighted many of the issues that may arise when institutional information becomes widely available.

Urban Universities. The literature on urban universities points out the failures of traditional measures in capturing the distinctiveness of urban universities. These measures tend to rely on a model of higher education that predates the inception of urban universities during the post–World War II period (Lynton, 1995). Urban universities have many features in common. They tend to have metropolitan or regional missions, enroll largely nontraditional students, offer a variety of course scheduling and extended programs, employ large numbers of adjunct and part-time faculty, and have a strong emphasis on community engagement. Learning goals at these institutions, however, tend to be similar to those at more traditional institutions, although the program mix may be somewhat different.

For many years, urban universities have been seeking ways to clarify their distinctiveness to the higher education community and the public and to define a common mission and identity. These institutions often have not fared well in national college rankings or legislative arenas, in part because it has been difficult to describe them accurately using traditional measures. The UUPP focused on electronic institutional portfolios as useful tools for capturing this distinctiveness. By combining numerical data with detailed examples of student and faculty work, campus programs and initiatives, or community involvement, the portfolios provided a multidimensional view of how campus programs and activities are related to institutional mission.

Direct evidence of student and faculty work provided context and meaning to the statistical information and narratives normally provided in accreditation self-studies. They also allowed the institutions to clarify and document how well they were serving their missions and achieving campus-specific goals.

Implementation Issues

Among UUPP participants, implementation of the portfolio project varied according to organizational structure, technological sophistication, and political climate. Although the project had not concluded at the time of this writing, several elements necessary for successful implementation had become evident: strong, explicit support from institutional leaders, a clearly articulated vision and plan for completion of the portfolio, availability of technological and artistic resources, inclusion of faculty in decision making, the direct involvement of institutional research, and involvement of the community and other external stakeholders in shaping the portfolio design and content.

Faculty Role. Several UUPP campuses involved faculty directly in the development of their portfolios. Faculty were active in advisory groups, departmental meetings, and small group discussions focused on the development of central messages for the portfolios and identification of relevant content. The inclusion of faculty at the core of portfolio design and development proved beneficial for both the faculty and their institutions. The faculty reported that involvement in the project provided them with the opportunity to learn more about what was happening outside their departments or programs and to gain a clearer picture of how their work was connected to institutional goals and priorities. Their active role in the portfolio process also sparked a renewed interest in assessment at their institutions, serving as an example of the following: "Faculty leaders knowledgeable about outcomes assessment can and should take the lead in educating peers about assessment, in setting up institutional structures that facilitate the planning process, and in guiding assessment initiatives toward institutional change" (Morse and Santiago, 2000, p. 33). Faculty involvement in the portfolios helped to initiate campus-wide conversations surrounding planning priorities, the purpose and use of assessment information, and the role of faculty in shaping a strategic direction for their institutions.

Institutional Research Role. Implementation of the project was enhanced by these campuses' well-defined institutional research functions, led by individuals who recognized the importance of adapting institutional research to the new realities of higher education: a complex decision-making environment, accelerated technological change, increased competition for students combined with declining financial support, and a new emphasis on student-centered approaches to teaching and learning. As writers on the topic have said, institutional researchers must reach beyond their traditional data collection and reporting roles to function as "information architects, change agents, and consultants of choice within their respective institutions" (Matier, Sidle, and Hurst, 1995, p. 76). They must work more closely with faculty in documenting the work of the institution, broadening the definition of "data" to include authentic examples of teaching, learning, research, and community engagement. Although providing information for decision support will continue to be an important function for institutional research, a large part of their work will involve collaboration and consultation with stakeholders within their institutions. As Matier, Sidle, and Hurst (1995) have written:

> Decision makers in this environment are linked more integrally with their constituents in making sense of the information provided to them. This information is processed jointly in the context of the particular institution's mission, vision, and values as well as its internal and external environments [p. 77].

Institutional researchers play an important role in the development of an institutional portfolio. They have a broad and detailed understanding of their campuses and maintain information on national trends in higher education, particularly those in accountability, assessment, and accreditation. Moreover, they are in a good position to understand which questions various users, both inside and outside the institution, ask of the data. Through their work, institutional researchers learn to understand the audiences for various kinds of information and have a good idea of who wants to know what about their institutions.

The Importance of Audience

Identification of audiences is an important step in the design of institutional portfolios. Development of a clear message, purpose, and focused selection of materials depends largely on the information needs of specific audiences. To be effective, a portfolio needs to address internal and external stakeholders' questions. Not only does the thoughtful identification of audiences help focus materials included in the portfolio, it is essential for effective Web-based communication. Web users move quickly through sites, taking their cues from visual imagery and descriptors. In order to attract the interest and attention of those who might wish to use it, the portfolio's message and purpose need to be described clearly.

Although electronic communication may be used to reach multiple audiences, Web developers suggest identifying a limited number of audiences and then targeting a site's content to their needs and interests. Possible audiences for information about public colleges and universities are numerous, from parents and prospective students to citizens concerned about education or state government expenditures. What can institutions do to identify audiences and determine their information needs? How can institutions use electronic media to enhance communication of this information?

Involving the Public. Demands from the public for accountability in education most often focus on student achievement, financial management, and contributions to the economy and welfare of regions and localities. Reports of test scores from primary and secondary students appear regularly in newspapers, and accounts of financial mismanagement or teachers' salary disputes frequently make headlines. Public higher education is not exempt from such scrutiny. Taxpayer revolts in many states have limited available revenue from general fund sources, placing state and local agencies, including higher education, in competition with one another for declining dollars. In response, some states have designed performance indicator systems to provide accountability data to legislatures and the public. These often ignore student learning outcomes as measures of performance, although accrediting associations have recognized the importance of outcomes as an indicator of institutional quality and effectiveness.

The public is interested, too, in concrete information that learning is taking place in public colleges and universities. Parents looking for a place to send their children to college, prospective adult students, and taxpayers expect graduates to be able to contribute something to their communities and to society as a whole. Publications such as *U.S. News and World Report* attempt to meet this need for information through annual reports that rank institutions based on a number of traditional, quantitative measures. But these are used as a proxy for solid information about what students do and learn while in school and say nothing about the practical or life-enriching experiences that institutions provide for them.

How can an institution know that the questions it is posing or trying to answer through the portfolio are the right ones? How can it discover whether it is communicating the information, with its emphasis on assessment and self-reflection, clearly and effectively?

Involving external constituencies in the development of institutional portfolios can provide a way to meet the public's need for information beyond facts and figures. The UUPP institutions used various methods to include the public and community stakeholders in the project. Early on, project participants developed a long list of possible audiences. It included accrediting associations, legislators and governing boards, citizens, other institutions, prospective and enrolled students, parents, faculty, alumni, and the general public. Each campus decided on the best method for including the perspectives of these audiences in the portfolio. Some elected to work with university advisory councils, comprising external stakeholders drawn from their urban or regional communities. Others involved community or business representatives, members of their accrediting associations, or students and alumni as members of their project implementation teams.

Perhaps the most important technique was the use of focus groups, interviews, and meetings with representatives of the portfolios' audiences. This technique played an important role in selecting, reviewing, and refining content. In some cases, project team members met individually with key stakeholders to go through the site page by page. In other cases, advisory committees met periodically with campus teams and then submitted comments electronically between meetings. Within the UUPP project, institutional review board members served as external auditors of campus processes and Web site development. Quarterly meetings of project participants facilitated the exchange of ideas and served as another means for gathering input.

Language. In order to communicate effectively with the public and other external stakeholders, it is important to use language in a portfolio that is free from higher education jargon. Service-learning, for example, is a common phrase among colleges and universities, but it is less familiar to the public. The UUPP participants frequently debated use of the terms assessment or institutional effectiveness. A principle that emerged from these discussions is that any narratives, descriptors, or other text used in an institutional portfolio should be clear, concise, and phrased in everyday language. Some materials may be better communicated through video and audio media rather than narrative forms. To ensure that all users can take full advantage of the site, care must be taken to provide versions of the portfolio that can be accessible to those with disabilities.

Responding to Accrediting Boards. Electronic institutional portfolios can provide detailed accountability information in response to accrediting standards, as well as authentic examples of student learning and faculty research and scholarship. Accrediting board members should play an active role focusing the selection and inclusion of materials in portfolios. Direct evidence of how the institution is meeting standards set by the accrediting board may be combined with explicit examples of how assessment tools and techniques are applied to student work samples. In this way, accountability and learning outcomes information can be brought together to illustrate, rather than report, how the institution is ensuring quality and monitoring improvement.

Airing "Dirty Laundry" versus Assessment and Improvement

Campus project teams spent several sessions discussing how data unfavorable to the institution—so-called dirty laundry—should be handled in the portfolios. The discussions focused on the assessment and accountability objectives of the project and raised two important questions:

Are there constructive and self-reflective ways to present assessment information that may not demonstrate increases in learning or institutional effectiveness data that reveal declines in key areas?

How can an institution make decisions about what should or should not be displayed, and to whom?

Targeting Content. Several UUPP participants dealt with the issue of dirty laundry by focusing on the information needs of the portfolios' designated audiences. To discover what information various groups wanted to see in the portfolios, the campuses used focus groups, surveys, and interviews with representatives of their targeted audiences. Institutional researchers also were a useful source of information about the questions typically asked of institutional data. To help understand how potentially negative information in the portfolios was being conveyed, the institutions presented proposed portfolio content to audience representatives in exploratory sessions. Session participants were asked to discuss their interpretation of the information and how well the materials responded to their questions.

Another way to ensure the responsible use and interpretation of information in the portfolios was to pose questions of interest crafted through interaction with intended audiences. For example, the display of institutional effectiveness data on enrollment might begin with a question such as, "What is the ethnic mix of students at this institution?" followed by short narratives and graphs of demographic data. Downward or upward trends would be linked with other relevant information, such as overall enrollment or institutional initiatives in this area, providing a context for the trend. Yet another method used in the project was to include a "report card" of internal performance indicators that highlighted areas showing little or no improvement and provided an explanation of institutional initiatives designed to reverse these trends. Data, positive or potentially negative, were not left hanging without being set in a context or accompanied by clear goals for improvement.

Assessment and Improvement. Important to the overall effectiveness of communication to individuals outside the campus walls were conversations among UUPP faculty, staff, and administrators about unfavorable data and how these might be represented in the portfolios. In some cases, these conversations led to the development or enhancement of assessment or improvement processes within the institution. Indeed, one use for the portfolio might be as a place—either virtual or realized through committees or groups—where discussions about a variety of topics, including teaching, learning, and assessment, might be carried out. Electronic portfolios can include designated pages (bulletin boards or chat rooms) for on-line discussion of these issues. To ensure participation in these virtual discussions, the campus should plan to link them with roundtables, symposia, or other campus gatherings that can be continued through discussion on the Web site.

Any institutional effectiveness data included in an institutional portfolio should be accompanied by information regarding how the institution is evaluating and using them for self-reflection and improvement. It is no longer good enough to present information related to the mission and goals of the institution to various publics without including an assessment and accountability component. If "dirty laundry" is left to hang without evidence of what the campus intends to do with it, it will lack context and meaning for both internal and external users of the data and be subject to misinterpretation or misuse.

Confidentiality and Use of Authentic Work

The term authentic evidence describes portfolio content. One form of authentic evidence is student work samples gathered from courses or programs—for example, drafts, rewrites, and final copies of written assignments; lab notebooks or other evidence of work on scientific or field experiments; PowerPoint presentations; videotaped speeches; and three-dimensional models of design projects. Several issues surround the decision to include student work samples in the portfolio; chief among these is the issue of confidentiality.

Informed Consent. Most campuses have institutional review boards responsible for overseeing the protection of human subjects in research. Informed consent is a key piece of research involving human subjects, even if that research does no physical or psychological harm to its participants. Although campus review boards did not view institutional portfolios as research, informed consent was seen as a useful tool for ensuring that those who provided examples of their work, participated in interviews, or were videotaped in meetings or other groups understood exactly what they were participating in, how the information would be used, and whom they could contact if they had questions.

Including Assessment Results. The issue of whether to include assessment results in addition to plans or descriptions of goals, objectives, and measures touches on both confidentiality and the issue of "dirty laundry." What is the institution's responsibility to its multiple publics to provide detailed assessments of student work? While the interests of various audiences may overlap, clearly some have interests or needs that others do not. It is possible to provide more detail for certain users than for others or to frame information in such a way that users can select how much detail they may wish to view. Decisions to employ confidential pages or to make assessment results widely available should be made carefully and with the full participation of faculty and institutional leaders.

Collecting and Organizing Information. Ease in navigation is an important feature of successful Web sites, so care must be taken not to make access to portfolio materials too complicated or unwieldy. In the UUPP electronic institutional portfolios, "data" ranged from numerical reports, tables, charts, and graphs to videotaped or audiotaped interviews with students and faculty. Institutional research fact books containing numerical information about the institution over a period of time were available as virtual links on the Web.

An important limitation of fact books generally is that they often include little in the way of analysis or interpretation and do not always frame their data tables within a larger context. For the purposes of an electronic institutional portfolio, it may be desirable to provide a virtual link to the institutional research Web site but also to provide data drawn from fact book tables in formats, such as narrative or graphics, that are more understandable to the public. Many portfolio users may be put off by rows and columns of numerical information and prefer more concise, focused representations of key facts. Again, involving constituents in the selection of materials for inclusion in the portfolio may help to focus and organize a portfolio's content.

Using Virtual Links. Many faculty and students, as well as programs and departments, maintain extensive Web sites that document their work. Most of the UUPP portfolios included virtual links to these pages as part of their content. As the campuses discovered, not everything needs to reside directly on portfolio pages; a simple narrative introduction can lead users to well-developed sites that contain the information they seek. The use of virtual links, however, should be used strategically rather than dominate portfolio content. These links also proved useful in displaying the technical competence of faculty and students in using the Web.

Conclusion

Electronic institutional portfolios can provide easy access for accrediting boards and the public to information about an institution's achievement of student learning outcomes and quality improvement efforts. As the UUPP institutions learned through their experiences, electronic portfolios can either substitute for traditional self-study reports or augment them with detailed examples of how standards are being met. They provide for a rich and in-depth portrayal of assessment and accountability information that goes beyond what can be included in a printed self-study report. Inclusion of stakeholders in the development of portfolios and the selection of materials for inclusion is key to their success as public communication tools. Issues such as confidentiality and the airing of unfavorable information, as well as technical issues such as ease of navigation, should receive careful consideration. Innovations in the way institutions provide information on their activities may lead to a better understanding of the connections between student learning and institutional effectiveness.

The growth of the Internet and wireless communication has pushed technology forward at a rapid rate. Some futurists predict that the Web will be replaced in the near future with more advanced forms of electronic communication. Electronic institutional portfolios are still in their infancy, and colleges and universities are just beginning to take advantage of the possibilities they offer. As accreditors and the public become more frequent users of Web-based information, electronic portfolios may replace more common forms of documenting institutional accountability and performance. Examples provided by the UUPP may pave the way for future advances in the use of Web applications among colleges and universities.

References

Kahn, S. "Electronic Institutional Portfolios." In S. Kahn (ed.), *Institutional Portfolios*. Forthcoming.

Lynton, E. A. "What Is a Metropolitan University?" In D. M. Johnson and D. A. Bell (eds.), *Metropolitan Universities: An Emerging Model in American Higher Education*. Denton: University of North Texas Press, 1995.

Matier, M. W., Sidle, C. C., and Hurst, P. J. "Institutional Researchers' Roles in the Twenty-First Century." In T. R. Sanford (ed.), *Preparing for the Information Needs of the Twenty-First Century*. New Directions for Institutional Research, no. 85. San Francisco: Jossey-Bass, 1995.

Morse, J. A., and Santiago, G., Jr. "Accreditation and Faculty: Working Together." *Academe: Bulletin of the American Association of University Professors*, 2000, *86*, 30-34.

Sanford, T. "Higher Education and Institutional Research: What Lies Ahead." In T. R. Sanford (ed.), *Preparing for the Information Needs of the Twenty-First Century*. New Directions for Institutional Research, no. 85. San Francisco: Jossey-Bass, 1995.

KATHI A. KETCHESON is director of institutional research and planning at Portland State University. She is also Portland State University campus project director for the Urban Universities Portfolio Project.

7

Meaningful change through the self-study process requires agreement about the mission of the institution and an understanding of faculty and administrative culture.

The Self-Study as a Chariot for Strategic Change

Rebecca R. Martin, Kathleen Manning, Judith A. Ramaley

Despite debates about the effectiveness of strategic change (Mintzberg, 1994), colleges and universities are determined to chart their futures, solidify their mission statements, decide resource allocations, and guide policy-making. This chapter discusses a strategic change process conducted at the University of Vermont (UVM). Eschewing the usual means of strategic change, the institution's leadership collaborated with faculty, staff, and students to use the accreditation process as a catalyst, or chariot (Clark, 1989, p. 7), for institutional transformation. The specific purposes of the strategic change processes were to

> engage a diverse cross section of the UVM community in the cultivation, exploration, and analysis of ideas and issues important to the University's future. . . . The process is designed to supplement ongoing efforts of governance bodies, academic and administrative departments, colleges, schools, and other entities and their leaders to improve quality and build a sustainable future for UVM [University of Vermont, 1999b].

The self-study process was designed to create the impetus for strategic change and establish a foundation on which to build a set of common goals and purposes that would unite the disparate experiences, values, methodologies, and worldviews of the disciplines. Effective assessment depends on the fact that "clarity and agreement on organizational mission are usually considered a fundamental principle for establishing systems of accountability" (Birnbaum, 1991, p. 10). Leadership from this premise involves determining how clarity and agreement can be achieved in academic organizations with the following characteristics:

They are loosely coupled (Weick, 1976).
Their administrative and faculty cultures are built on incompatible decision-making models and epistemological structures (Birnbaum, 1989).
They contain core memberships that are discipline centered, fragmented, and specialized (Clark, 1983; Weick, 1976).
They are made up of individuals and groups who are frustrated about their inability to affect institutional priorities (Birnbaum, 1991).
They experience difficulty teaching and empowering smart people how to learn (Argyris, 1991).

A divide of culture and experience exists between faculty and administrative views of organizational change. Faculty often view administrators as bureaucratic, unscholarly, business minded, impatient with faculty concerns, and insensitive to academic values. For their part, administrators see faculty as conservative, suspicious of the administration, reluctant to change, unwilling to contribute to the daily operations of the institution, and, in some cases, cynical about whether any change is either possible or desirable. We believe that common ground must be created in order to bring together and use the talents and energies of both cultures to promote meaningful, mission-related institutional change. The occasion of the institutional self-study and reaffirmation of regional accreditation provided an opportunity to test this hypothesis.

Change Toward Democratic Learning Organizations

Our approach to institutional reaccreditation is based on new kinds of inter-action—shared governance, faculty and administrative collaboration, joint decision making—and dialogue within a loosely coupled system. These activities bring the different elements of university subcultures together into one intellectual, democratic, united academic community where decisions are approached through the exercise of collective responsibility in shared governance.

In such a community, each person can do his or her best work as well as develop as an educated human being. These goals can occur regardless of the role played within the organization: student, faculty, staff, administrator, trustee, or advisory board member. This growth and achievement is most likely to be accomplished within an environment of clear purposes and shared responsibility, necessary conditions for any meaningful accountability and assessment.

To accomplish the goals of an institutional democracy where learning is predominant, a university must become a true learning organization (Senge, 1990). According to Garvin, "A learning organization is . . . skilled at creating, acquiring, interpreting and transferring knowledge, and at modifying its behavior to reflect new knowledge and insights" (1993, p. 78). In a learning organization, change is intentional, based on a valid body of knowledge, and rigorously assessed. That is, change is a scholarly act. To develop the capacities of a learning organization, support collaborative behavior, and establish a scholarly basis for action, a university community must accomplish six tasks:

1. Instill a discipline of reflection and a culture of evidence, insisting that everyone support his or her perspectives with information (qualitatively and quantitatively derived), not just opinions.
2. Create new patterns of conversation and interaction that encourage and support everyone's involvement in defining the essential issues in a learning organization and transformative institution.
3. Engage in genuine conversation about difficult and controversial subjects as one way to disperse power and leadership throughout the organization. These conversations promote discipline and clarity of purpose rather than confusion about goals and actions.
4. Adopt a philosophy of experimentation, assessment, and management of reasonable risks.
5. Create new ways to access information and a common base of acceptable knowledge about the institution and its performance and condition. This activity encourages everyone to make informed choices among the many options.
6. Create legitimacy for planning and assessment by documenting the research and practice from which the approaches are derived. In the process of creating a research-based foundation for action, the different norms and standards of knowledge espoused by the disciplines making up the academic community must be understood, subcultures defined and recognized, and common and agreed-on standards developed to guide good decision making.

The leader in a learning organization builds a shared vision, surfaces and challenges prevailing mental models, fosters systemic patterns of thinking, and models intellectual virtues. These virtues include "the willingness to explore widely, the ability to test one's ideas against those of others, the capacity to listen thoughtfully, and the strength to adduce reasons for one's assertions" (Payne, 1996, p. 19). These capacities cannot be exercised just at the top of an organization but must be widely distributed throughout the organization.

A learning organization with a value for shared leadership is psychologically safe. People within such a setting believe that they are wanted and belong, valued so that ideas and thoughts are listened to and used, and respected and free from harassment and discriminatory behavior. They also feel empowered to share responsibility for achieving institutional goals and purposes, are comfortable and knowledgeable enough to make decisions in areas of responsibility, and share in a vision for the future. They also respect each other's expertise. As one considers the task outlined above, the organizational model of loosely coupled systems can provide some insight.

We assume that universities, particularly large ones, are loosely coupled organizations, defined by Weick (1976, 1979) as possessing few strong variables in common. UVM, whose experience is shared here as a case study, exemplifies a particularly potent form of loose coupling. The campus possesses a highly decentralized structure exacerbated in the 1980s and 1990s by budget cuts that encouraged territoriality and rigid college, school, and department structures. A decade of frequent turnover in senior leadership served to intensify this situation. In addition to loose coupling among academic units, long-term mission idiosyncrasies allowed university members to argue that the institution is both public and private. The resulting highly decentralized structure contains some pockets only tangentially related to the institution's core mission.

Interactions of Administrative and Faculty Culture

Fundamental to understanding and launching a change initiative is to recognize the differences in decision-making conventions, time frames, priorities, and constituents of faculty and administrative cultures.

Administrative Culture. Efficiency, competence, effectiveness, productivity, and accountability characterize collegiate administrative culture today. Whether originating in the faculty ranks or undergoing professional preparation specifically for leadership positions, administrators occupy a unique culture in higher education. They work within a hierarchical organizational structure of loosely coupled offices and departments, exercise power emanating from their position within that hierarchy, focus on goal- and mission-oriented activities, are responsible for particular responsibilities and services, and lack tenure. In times of retrenchment, administrators look to change the institution to relieve financial pressure (Alpert, 1986; Birnbaum, 1989). Recent advances on campus have left administrators more technologically savvy than faculty, as well as proficient with information sources and data. Both of these emerging characteristics of administrative culture provide individuals with an institution-wide perspective that is often lacking in faculty culture.

In administrative culture, decision making is ultimately top down, although it is often conducted in collaboration with faculty, student, and staff constituencies. The buck still stops in the president's or provost's office. Benchmarking, accountability, and strategic planning are priorities (Birnbaum, 1991; Lenington, 1996). While some view "collegiate institutions that are dominated by the managerial cultures . . . [as] repressive, uninspired, places to work or learn" (Berquist, 1996, p. 65), ineffective management exposes a campus to diminished resources, poor planning, and mission creep.

Administrative culture has expanded by adding layers of control, usually in response to external regulatory mandates. The jurisdiction and role of administrators have increased as they assumed responsibilities previously exercised by faculty (such as advising). Increased numbers of staff have been hired to handle this expansion. Mirroring the disciplines, administrative culture is growing more specialized, with identities and unique communities of interest (Kuh and Whitt, 1988).

Despite this administrative expansion, executive leadership has lost significant control in recent years for an array of reasons—for example:

- The politicization and polarization of governing boards
- The increasing span of control of senior administrators as administrative functions have become more complex
- External mandates and criticisms from legislatures and governors
- The priorities of external funding agencies

Finally, increasing interest of and scrutiny by external constituencies, including parents, public citizens, and community members, complicate this already complex administrative situation and subject the institution and its administration to a growing number of stakeholders who wish to shape the agenda and priorities of the institution.

Traditional Faculty Culture. Clark (1963, 1989) and others describe traditional faculty culture as emphasizing peer review, collegial relationships, self-governance, curriculum preeminence, and a hierarchy of disciplines, among other features. Faculty culture is organized around bodies of knowledge rather than administrative tasks. Clark (1963) described two kinds of faculty: *locals,* who locate their professional effort within the institution, and *cosmopolitans,* who have little institutional loyalty but a strong discipline and, to a limited extent, home department orientation.

Classical faculty culture possesses the following characteristics and priorities: autonomy, collegiality, peer review, self-governance, and primacy of scholarship. Faculty members place an extraordinary emphasis on the pursuit and dissemination of knowledge. This knowledge is represented in disciplines with separate knowledge traditions, thought categories, standards of proof, modes of inquiry, norms of scholarly expression, and codes of conduct. These codes are "hard to pin down since they are only vaguely sensed by their members, and easily dismissed as romantic, self-serving portraits when articulated in speech or prose" (Clark, 1983, pp. 76–77).

Faculty members view their core professional membership to be the discipline in which they were educated and socialized. The disciplines are divided into various domains according to the presence or absence of a body of theory (hard versus soft); the presence or absence of concerns about the application of knowledge to practical problems (pure versus applied); and whether research is conducted on living or physical systems (humanistic versus scientific) (Biglan, 1973). This intense, and at times constricted, specialization results in a "high degree of fragmented professionalism" (Clark, 1983, p. 36). Therefore, faculty culture is paradoxically fractured by expertise yet underscored with the common values and characteristics described above.

Faculty decision making is not necessarily timely or mission driven. Collegiality, consensus building, and discussion mark faculty decision making that is in strong contrast to the data-driven, managerially derived, hierarchical decision making of administrators. Relying on disciplinary insights rather than local institutional conditions, each academic discipline has a different working definition of what it means to know something with sufficient certainty to act on that knowledge. From one discipline to another, the evidence needed to marshal belief and to justify action varies.

Faculty members from various disciplines make implicit assumptions about the means to find solutions to problems. These assumptions are rarely articulated but can be detected in the criticism that faculty level against planning activities. Specifically, humanities faculty members complain about language and underlying intentions. Social science faculty members comment about process and its legitimacy. They are especially critical if the theory and practice shared originated in business settings. In the sciences, complaints center on the data, question hidden hypotheses, or challenge a priori conclusions reflected in what information was collected and used. Faculty members across the disciplines are particularly suspicious of the standard administrative tools of rational decision making (Swenk, 1999).

Without mechanisms to reconcile the decision rules from the disciplines, administrators struggle to build a case for the legitimacy of either what is known or what should serve as a basis for action. Few faculty members acknowledge that administrative practices, including strategic planning or the establishment of accountability measures, are based on a legitimate body of knowledge derived from scholarly inquiry. Many substitute the practices and epistemological structures of their discipline to critique the planning exercises.

At large, complex colleges and universities, faculty divide themselves into smaller and smaller subcultures centered on departments and disciplines. Thus, larger institutions resemble academic holding companies. The locus of decision making becomes the smallest unit: the department or the school (Birnbaum, 1991). This characteristic can lead to a circumstance in which a sense of common purpose is subsumed by the uneasy sum of the expectations of each unit, loosely held together by the tradition and habits of the campus community. The goals of the institution are upstaged by a multiplicity of individual departmental and college priorities, with the following major consequences:

Uneven communication patterns isolate individual faculty members and prevent them from sharing responsibility for the common good, such as undergraduate education.
Diffused, dissipated, and diminished resources limit opportunities and strain faculty relationships.

Prevailing methods of evaluation and reward (such as overemphasis on research, indefensible salary differences, and superficial evaluation of teaching) undermine attempts to create an environment more conducive to faculty interaction (Massy, Wilger, and Colbeck, 1994).

As individuals and groups lose their ability to affect their institution and influence its priorities and direction, they "tend to assert their influence and status by acting as veto blocs" (Birnbaum, 1991, p. 15). The result is a blockage of change and maintenance of the status quo, the only condition not subject to someone's veto.

Collaborative Faculty Culture. Higher education organizations today occupy a world of diverse student populations, fierce competition, fast-paced technology, volatile financial climates, rapid change, and strained resources. What does faculty culture look like in these complex settings impatient with protracted decision making, isolated self-governance, and tightly defined disciplinary perspectives? Is it possible to take the significant strengths of traditional faculty cultures (such as monitoring curricular quality, creating high standards through peer review, and encouraging knowledge discovery) to create a new faculty culture without the problematic aspects (for example, conservative approaches to curriculum, reluctance to change, suspicion about administration, and minimal participation in institutional concerns)?

Newer organizational configurations require faculty who are locals *and* cosmopolitans. Reflecting the complexity of modern life, faculty must adapt a Janus-like approach to their teaching, scholarship, and service. Looking toward their disciplines, a rich array of approaches to knowledge can inform rather than interrupt a look in the opposite direction at institutional decision making. Who better than faculty can apply the critical thinking necessary for informed institutional planning?

Complex higher education communities can no longer afford to have faculty who view their jobs only from a disciplinary perspective or see the university from a faculty perspective. The complexity of the university, the presence of a volatile internal and external environment, and the existence of myriad issues necessitates the engagement and involvement of all community members in campuswide issues. Just as administrators in complex higher education organizations must competently sense the environment, respond to market demands, and harmonize constituency prerogatives with mission and purpose, new faculty culture can reconcile expansiveness over narrowness and institutional and disciplinary loyalty.

Because there is no single faculty culture, particularly in complex systems, the following characteristics of faculty of the future are offered in both a tentative and optimistic vein. Proponents of a new faculty culture would loosen their current overreliance on expert power. There would be more understanding about multiple approaches to learning. The lessons about connection and interrelationship learned from such disparate fields as physics and women's studies would encourage a more flexible, integrated approach to teaching, research, and service. With the recognition that the activities of a career ebb and flow, teaching, research, and service would be employed as tools rather than end goals, in flexible, perhaps forgiving ways to ensure a viable faculty career. New faculty culture would mirror the collaborative, empowered practices promoted by current feminist and organizational theorists (Helgesen, 1995). Distinctions regarding status would be blurred. A richer understanding of the mutually shaping processes of teaching, learning, and discovery would ensue.

A question pursued in this chapter and central to the strategic change process applied at UVM is, How do you get faculty members engaged in administrative activities that are (1) crucial to the institution (such as coherent curriculum, engaged students, clearer goals, and sustainable budget), (2) cannot be achieved without their support, and (3) are not traditionally viewed as within their purview? The self-study and the subsequent strategic change process were used as mechanisms to engender this involvement.

Faculty decision-making models that correspond with the governing board's and administration's need for expediency are not possible unless faculty governance acts as an effective mediator. Without effective faculty governance as this intermediary, the negative aspects of faculty culture (among them, suspicion, conservatism about and reluctance to change, and disengagement in daily campus operations) can hamper change and institutional transformation.

Empowering People to Learn in a Learning Organization

Another assumption underlying the perspectives in this chapter is that it is difficult to teach smart people how to learn. According to Argyris (1991), "Success in the marketplace increasingly depends on learning, yet most people don't know how to learn" (p. 99). Highly educated professionals tend to define learning as problem solving. They focus on looking for errors in the external environment rather than in their own work, and when decisions or other administrative action do not go well, they are likely to blame someone else or external circumstances beyond their control as the source of the problem.

In contrast, Argyris (1991) recommends that faculty and administrators, like other highly professional organizational members in other kinds of organizations, "need to reflect critically on their own behavior, identify ways they often inadvertently contribute to the organization's problems, and then change how they act" (p. 101). Critical reflection leading to learning is unlikely to happen in higher education because faculty members and senior administrators have been generally successful in what they do, have been validated for their past success by peers, and are inexperienced with failure. They simply do not know how to learn from it. In the face of internal difficulties, both faculty and administrators will become defensive, ignore criticism, discount evidence of failing quality or growing financial instability, and put the blame on someone else. Rather than embracing the learning that Argyris champions, neither group learns in a manner necessary for success in a complex modern organization. Recognizing this, UVM's leadership sought ways to stimulate involvement, engagement, transformation, and above all, learning.

Clark's "Chariots" and Organizational Transformation

Clark (1989) argued that the dream of common values and shared purpose that will integrate the desires and capacities of all the disciplines is no longer possible in today's complex and multidimensional institutions. He wrote, "As commonness recedes, we have to determine how 'unity in diversity' comes about. One path to such unity is normative systems that hook self-interest to larger institutional chariots" (p. 7). To transform the university, organizational leaders need to discover initiatives that are grand enough to serve as chariots that transcend faculty and disciplinary self-interests. Such chariots must capture the attention and energies of a contemporary faculty as well as administrators. In the process, they create a new kind of commitment to an academic community in the face of the boundaries to collegiality and shared purpose that are established by the disciplines, institutional complexity, and time constraints.

Chariots can also be thought of as *trigger events* (Isabella, 1992). These may be any perturbation or change in a loosely coupled system that sets off a pattern of new behaviors and thoughts among the members of the community. Such new behaviors and reflections occur as members try to understand what is happening and what it might mean for them personally and for their programs. By their nature, trigger events "unbalance established routines and evoke conscious thought on the part of organizational members" (Isabella, 1992, p. 19). Common trigger events are the appointment of a new president or provost, a financial crisis and attendant budget cuts, a new legislative mandate, or the reorganization of a school or college. Emanating from national sources or more locally generated, trigger events can also include curriculum reform to increase societal outreach and service-learning, a significant ideological or paradigm shift within a discipline, initiation of learning-centered curricula, or loss of public confidence.

Self-Study as a Trigger Event. If effectively handled, a process of institutional self-study can become a trigger event. This can occur if a campus community takes seriously its obligation to examine itself critically. Although regional associations differ in how they approach accreditation, we use the guidelines of the New England Association of Schools and Colleges (NEASC) to describe the scope of this work.

To document institutional quality, a NEASC self-study should make the case that the institution:

- Has clearly defined purposes appropriate to an institution of higher learning
- Has assembled and organized those resources necessary to achieve its purposes
- Is achieving its purposes
- Has the ability to continue to achieve its purposes

Accreditation processes also encourage the institution to improve its quality, increase its effectiveness, and strive continually for excellence. The self-study process is sufficiently profound, although simple, that it has the potential of unbalancing established organizational routines. This evokes conscious, reflective thought of organizational members and thus contributes to the development of the clarity and agreement essential to guiding institutional progress toward excellence.

The campus reaction to a trigger event unfolds in four predictable stages, each requiring different leadership responses:

- Stage 1. As rumors fly about change, members adopt a detective mind-set, assembling rumors and tidbits of information and often drawing sweeping inferences and conclusions from them. The management task at this stage is to promote open and honest discussion of fears and concerns and to provide accurate information to dispel rumors.
- Stage 2. Once a change begins, some members draw on traditional explanations and familiar patterns of the organization to explain what is happening and resist the change. At this point, the management task is to offer new and more constructive interpretations of what the changes mean.
- Stage 3. Once the change is implemented, people move into an "amended" mind-set as they search for the symbolic meaning of what has happened and what it portends for them personally. As they do so, they are "trying to actively reconstruct their environment: deciding what to retain and what to alter" (Isabella, 1992, p. 23).
- Stage 4. As the change progresses, managers and others review the consequences of what has taken place and publicly reinterpret what it means. People are doing their best to put the change in perspective. Unless this stage is actively managed, everyone will draw his or her own individual conclusions that may be at significant variance to the institution's mission and strategies.

The achievement of clarity and direction in a loosely coupled organization requires a major environmental change or mandate, such as a fiscal crisis that is honestly and openly addressed or the deliberate introduction of a significant internal imbalance. Whatever the cause of the destabilization, a successful outcome depends on consistent and open communication and leadership accessibility at each stage of the planning or change process. Leaders must consistently help people understand what is happening and what it means for the organization and for individuals. They need also to uncover and deal with rumors and misperceptions through open and honest dialogue.

The Self-Study Process as a Catalyst for Institutional Change: A Case History

Like many other institutions of higher education, UVM has been examining its priorities and considering its future for many years. In the past decade, three major planning processes have been undertaken. Led by different presidents, these planning exercises engaged similar issues and challenges: the need to define quality, make choices and focus efforts, and optimize the use of a declining base of resources. Although many topics were studied and numerous recommendations made, minimum actions were the result. The first two planning processes did not result in a shared understanding and agreement on the mission of the institution.

In 1997, President Judith Ramaley and provost Geoffrey Gamble selected the accreditation self-study process to launch a revitalized and inclusive planning effort. Its aim was to establish a coherent, consistent, and productive direction for the future of the university. The community discourse that began with the preparation of this self-study continued for three years, taking different forms and paths as issues and questions emerged and participants moved in and out of the conversation.

Setting the Foundation. An important foundation for this work and a tension underlying much of the dialogue was the link between planning and budgeting. This tension emanated from the need to stabilize the resource base for the institution. The use of strategic budgeting to address this link was clearly articulated in many settings—for example, "Strategic budgeting is really a means for building a sense of community and shared purpose and for translating these intentions into individual and collective goals, activities and responsibilities. Strategic budgeting is an investment model that emphasizes as its primary purpose the generation and preservation of assets that will support the university mission" (Ramaley, 1998, p. 11). Not surprisingly, the community discourse most clearly perceived as linked to changes in resource allocation created the strongest interest and concern throughout the change process.

Angelo's (1999) approach to curricular change proved helpful in creating a learning community within our loosely coupled system. Four stages in this process are posited:

1. Build shared trust: begin by lowering social and interpersonal barriers to change.
2. Build shared motivation: collectively identify goals worth working toward and problems worth solving.
3. Build a shared language: develop a collective understanding of new concepts (mental models) needed for transformation.

4. Build shared guidelines: develop a short list of research-based guidelines for using assessments to promote learning, or by analogy, to measure institutional progress toward its goals.

These stages are certainly overlapping, and UVM's success in achieving these outcomes was mixed at best. However, the construct helps us understand the underlying motivations for the process.

Building Shared Trust. The self-study process offered the first major opportunity for the UVM community to engage broadly the agenda that President Ramaley set forth in her inaugural address (Ramaley, 1997). The Areas of Emphasis option, an alternative approach to self-study offered by the NEASC to allow institutions to focus on specific questions and issues, was chosen to bring together internal and external constituencies to consider six broad areas of institutional focus. This served not only the time-limited purposes of completing the study, but began a longer-term process of vetting, modifying, and evolving the concepts discussed to position the university better for the next decade (University of Vermont, 1999a). Following a participatory process to develop a new mission statement for the university, campuswide forums and focused roundtable discussions were held on the following themes:

- UVM and Its Students in the 21st Century
- UVM and Its Faculty and Staff in the 21st Century
- Research and Scholarship at UVM in the 21st Century
- UVM, Vermont, and the World in the 21st Century
- The Measurement of Quality and Effectiveness at UVM in the 21st Century
- Strategic Budgeting in the 21st Century

These broad-based discussions and the resulting sections of the self-study report generated ideas, developed themes, posed questions, and proposed directions for further consideration. Further discussions among several groups of university leaders drawn from administration, faculty governance, and trustees generated two consistent themes: the need for greater communication and collaboration and the need to act. Thus, although a new sense of shared trust did not emerge as a result of these considerations, some barriers to change were softened, and the possibility of movement was entertained. The degree of urgency, however, varied from very high among trustees to moderate among many faculty and staff.

Building Shared Motivation. In order to engage a larger segment of the university community in the process of considering the future and its challenges, the university worked with Rod Napier, an organizational consultant specializing in collaborative strategic planning processes. The UVM Strategic Change Process used large and small group designs (Napier, Sidle, and Sanaghan, 1998) to stimulate conversation and reflection, as well as to increase the community's openness to change. Over the course of four months, more than 1,450 faculty, staff, students, trustees, and alumni engaged in dialogue and discussion on issues key to sustaining UVM and strengthening its programs. Rather than focusing on decisions, the process was designed to expand, inform, and improve the thinking of those responsible for decisions by engaging a large number of participants in discussing critical topics and concerns. This process was led by a broad-based steering group appointed by the president, with responsibility for overseeing, guiding, and facilitating the strategic change process.

The heart of the process was a series of small group interactions based on ten themes derived from the self-study reports. These general topic areas were selected from among the many issues facing UVM because of their key relationship to the university's ability to reach a sustainable, strategic budget:

• Attracting quality students
• Affording academic quality
• Student needs and interests
• Research and scholarship
• Graduate education
• Student retention
• Compensation and performance
• Support services/staffing the university
• Utilization of facilities
• Information technology

For each of these topics, mixed groups of faculty, staff, students, and trustees discussed critical questions. The discussions were structured to give each participant an equal voice, regardless of status or organizational position (Napier, Sidle, and Sanaghan, 1998). Questions were crafted by the steering group in advance of these sessions, and facilitators drawn from the faculty and staff were trained to lead these events.

The purposes of this phase were to gather information, test the assumptions on which options would be developed and assessed, and begin to generate options based on knowledge about the university. The process was designed to draw the shared experience and knowledge of campus community members. The results of these meetings were synthesized, posted on the university Web site, and reviewed by governance groups and several administrative bodies.

Throughout this period, those administering the process received several challenges to the strategic change process. The topics under consideration, the background data provided to support the discussions, and the individuals leading the effort were criticized. Some questions from community members challenged the process itself:

- What connection does all of this activity have to decision making?
- Can you prove rigorously and scientifically that this new process is valid?
- Why can't we define and study the questions first?
- How can we express opinions without proper examination of all of the evidence?
- How can such a consultative process generate enough substantive information to support good decisions?

Other questions addressed the motives of the leaders:

- Why are you asking us to move so fast?
- Is there a hidden hand at work here?
- If there is no hidden hand, are we simply adrift?
- Have we exhausted all alternatives to change?
- Why don't you just raise more money from donors and leave us alone?

On the other hand, many individuals came forward quietly to express their gratitude for the opportunity to be involved and their support for change. The beginnings of shared motivation for change were seen as common articulations of goals and problems emerged.

Building Shared Language. On the basis of the ideas generated in the small group discussions, the steering group selected eight topics for more in-depth exploration by key stakeholders at two day-long conferences, each with over one hundred participants drawn from all segments of the university community. Small groups developed recommendations for further study, created criteria for selecting among competing options, identified possible consequences of various options, and developed the capacity to make institutional choices. Again, the results of these meetings were synthesized and posted on the Web site.

At this stage, perspectives coalesced around several key points. Some themes were heard every time a particular topic was discussed, the most pervasive of which was a desire for action (University of Vermont, 2000). The following topics reflect the major recommendations articulated by the community:

- Improve teaching and advising
- Improve the sense of community at UVM
- Expand and enrich our focus on diversity and global perspectives
- Focus curricular offerings as appropriate to mission and strategic directions
- Refine and improve our service orientation and responsiveness to multiple constituencies
- Enhance the academic culture for students and create a tighter connection between residential life and academic life
- Increase compensation for faculty and staff, creating closer ties between merit increases and compensation

- Reassess graduate education
- Improve communication both within the university and to constituents outside the university
- Invest in information technology
- Create a comprehensive system to monitor and understand space needs and resources

The steering group developed thirty-two recommendations from the four months of small group interactions and forwarded them to the president and provost for consideration. These recommendations were action oriented and, where appropriate, included specific time frames, accountability measures, and responsible individuals. Some recommendations identified the need for involvement of campus governance groups. In several cases, targeted work groups of faculty, staff, and students were gathered to investigate an issue and develop concrete recommendations based on that analysis. Other recommendations were presented with the expectation that leadership would modify them as specific implementation plans were developed.

The information gathered through this extended period of community discourse was culled and evaluated. A shared language developed around issues of academic quality, the student experience, and sustainable resources. Imagining models that would lead to institutional transformation proved more difficult, especially in areas where such thinking directly challenged the status quo.

Building Shared Guidelines. The wealth of community-based wisdom gathered throughout the strategic change process was combined with other institutional change components, such as a position management system, academic program review, and a strategic budgeting process to create a draft strategic plan. Criteria were established to evaluate options and measure progress:

- Will this decision preserve and enhance quality?
- Will this decision focus the university on what it does best and what will make us distinctive?
- Are these activities or programs critical to the mission and worthy of investment?
- Will this investment or change increase the perceived and actual value of the UVM experience for students, faculty, and staff?
- Will this effort help us create a sustainable resource base for the future?
- Above all, is this in the best interests of our students?

To reach the goals, strategic steps must be taken to implement the vision, as well as create a stable resource base as a foundation for future success. As the university community faces the prospect of investing in the future within the constraints of present budgetary challenges, many people are experiencing a particularly difficult disconnect between the promise of strategic planning and the realities of strategic budgeting.

The challenge of creating excellence and a sustainable budget will be met through redesign, reengineering, and reduction of support services; elimination of redundancy in academic programs and offerings; reduction of courses and majors with low demand; and focus on mission-critical activities. At the same time, new and expanded revenue sources will be sought to help meet university objectives. For the first year of the strategic plan, this will be primarily a cost-cutting exercise. In subsequent years, strategic investments will become increasingly apparent in furtherance of the goals set for the community.

An essential element in the success of this process will be thoughtful, cohesive planning at all levels, linked directly to the university context outlined in the self-study and strategic plan. Development of department and unit plans will be coordinated with college, school, and division strategies and linked to the goals and objectives of the UVM strategic plan.

Lessons Learned. Designed from the outset as part of a larger strategic change agenda, UVM's self-study process was a valuable chariot to carry campuswide thinking and discussion about the university's future. The preparation of the report and the visit of the accrediting team were perhaps not as important as what the university community learned about itself along the way.

In the interest of developing the clarity and agreement on organizational mission discussed at the outset of this chapter, we engaged many voices in this discourse, often with unexpected results. Our intent was to establish a framework for this dialogue and then to let the natural wisdom of the community guide the development of the themes, ideas, and options. The ambiguity, uncertainty, and lack of control inherent in this approach placed new demands on institutional leadership and required new understandings from community members. Placing trust in the community is often a challenge for leaders, but at times in this process, it appeared even harder for the community to trust itself.

Learning About the Institution. The strategic change process placed a great deal of stress on the university. The process exacerbated the structural imbalance found in loosely coupled systems. Open discussion was encouraged across organizational boundaries, people from many levels were encouraged to participate, and intense consideration of new ways of thinking was promoted. When combined with the open deliberations on the worsening fiscal condition of the institution, the stage was set for the destabilization that may lead, if properly managed, to substantive change.

As the leadership and the community reflected on the responses, the form and nature of resistance to change became more transparent. Everyone learned a great deal about the institutional culture. The patterns of response illuminated the traditional sources of power, especially among the faculty and the colleges. Communication channels were clarified when various trigger events stimulated rumors and information flow. Interpreters emerged who shaped the discourse in positive and negative ways as the conversations unfolded. The prospect of real institutional change challenged common assumptions about how UVM works, including the following:

- We cannot invest in the future while simultaneously reducing our current budgets.
- We cannot redesign programs or do things differently without degrading quality.
- Our differences from other institutions of higher education make the proposed changes impossible, unrealistic, or absurd.
- Trend data and other forms of quantitative information are not valid if they are contrary to our common understandings or to our personal experiences.

Understanding and addressing the concerns that underlie these assumptions moved the difficult task of finding common ground forward, although the final results of this work have yet to be assessed.

The Intersection of Institutional Cultures. Differences in organizational subcultures highlighted the change process as it intensified. While it was easy to attribute faculty reaction to basic resistance to change or administrative positions to a lack of understanding, a closer look at the tensions inherent in the differing perspectives presented a more complex picture.

Principal among these tensions was the debate over the curriculum, a core element in the definition of faculty roles and responsibilities. As administrators raised questions regarding the resource base available to support an expansive array of academic offerings, faculty members countered with concerns regarding essential elements of a comprehensive education. The disciplinary principles and values intrinsic to faculty perspectives were frequently at odds with the viewpoints held by administrators based on the needs of employers and the marketplace. These disparities meant that the conversations regarding changes in academic programs often resulted in conflict and debate.

Two areas of tension were educational quality and student success. Senior administrators responding to pressures from governing boards, policymakers, and business leaders saw accountability and productivity as prominent concerns. For them, success was measured socially and contextually across all fields of study. For faculty members grounded in specific disciplines, quality was assessed according to the standards of a domain of knowledge extending throughout academe. Thus, the questions administrators raised regarding the need for assessment and accountability were heard by faculty members as challenges to the excellence of their programs. At the same time, administrators saw faculty adhering to discipline-specific definitions of quality as unresponsive to a changing environment.

Another area of debate was over the role of service and engagement in the mission of the university. This emerged as a tension among faculty cultures as well as between some faculty and the senior administration. On one side of this debate was a fundamental view that the work of the university must have a direct impact on society. On the other was the belief that the university is a collegium of scholars creating ideas to contribute to the world of knowledge. In each of these tensions, elements of both perspectives were essential to the future of the university. Creating the opportunity for both sides to be heard and understood and for balance among seemingly competing views was crucial to the university's ongoing success.

The commonalities in responding to change across institutional cultures are as important to note as the differences. Irrespective of cultural perspective, faculty, administrators, and students share the difficulties of dealing with ambiguity and uncertainty brought about by significant organizational change. Although it is clear that strategic change in this environment must be a continuous learning process, the desire for predictability and stability is very strong. By respecting and valuing the different perspectives contributed from the various UVM cultures, we hope to preserve what is most important about our institution while strengthening the foundation on which it functions.

Creation of a Learning Organization and Shared Governance. Through the self-study and the strategic change process, UVM's leadership endeavored to create a learning organization. They have sought to foster a culture where "smart people can learn" from their experiences and recognize and respond in meaningful ways to internal and external needs and expectations. The exercise of leadership in a learning organization is like every other experience within a group or organization. It is shaped by how well the interactions and communication patterns of leaders throughout the organization interpret the experience of the organization and thereby create meaning and direction for other members of the campus community. The climate or environment created within an organization is also affected by the leader's expectations and the attitudes of faculty and staff toward campus leaders and the administration.

The distributed mode of leadership in a learning organization is encouraged at UVM. Those most uncomfortable with the directions that the resulting change might take have questioned the approach and called for more direct, authoritarian decision making. Instead, the community is being challenged to do what Heifetz calls "adaptive work"—facing problems for which there are no simple, painless solutions, problems that require us to learn in new ways (1994, p. 2).

The experience described here suggests that the definition of shared governance in a university setting is changing from one distinguished by separation of powers to a relationship based on genuinely collaborative problem-solving activities. This new alliance is characterized by more open access to information, collaboration during the formative stages of identifying issues and options, thoughtful discussion of the principles on which a choice will be made and success measured, and evaluation of various possibilities through the perspectives of the different organizational subcultures and academic disciplines. While the moment of actual choice is not always shared, the path to decision has taken a new form.

Conclusion

The accreditation self-study at UVM was used as a catalyst for a university strategic change process. This work was grounded in three basic premises: (1) meaningful change and effective assessment strategies must be based on both clarity and agreement about the mission of the institution; (2) clarity of purpose requires effective communication within and across the subcultures that constitute a campus community; and (3) within the loosely coupled sub-cultures and programs of a university, open and honest communication among the academic disciplines and between faculty and administration will occur only if a perturbing or trigger event unsettles the campus community enough to create new patterns of thought and new behavior on the part of a significant proportion of the faculty, staff, and administration.

The resulting campuswide process of reflection and exploration of options for the future can make new demands on all participants and reveal underlying aspects of the campus culture that limit any process of effective communication and inhibit transformational change. These cultural barriers to the achievement of clarity and direction can be reduced by:

1. Instilling a discipline of reflection and a culture of evidence that supports honest discussions about the current condition of the institution
2. Fostering new patterns of conversation and interaction that encourage and support the involvement of a broad spectrum of the campus community in defining the future and assessing institutional progress toward shared goals
3. Promoting genuine conversation about difficult and controversial subjects as a way to disperse power and leadership throughout the organization
4. Advancing a philosophy of experimentation, assessment, and management of reasonable risks associated with change
5. Providing open access to meaningful information about the condition and resource base of the institution
6. Approaching planning as a scholarly endeavor that creates a research-based foundation for action.

By its nature, a well-designed strategic change process triggered by an effective self-study can incorporate these principles and make change itself a scholarly act[1] built on the strengths of both administrative culture and traditional faculty culture.

Note

The authors are indebted to Michael Reardon of Portland State University and Barbara Holland of the Office of University Partnerships, U.S. Housing and Urban Development.

References

Alpert, D. "Performance and Paralysis: The Organizational Context of the American Research University." *Journal of Higher Education,* 1986, *56*(3), 241–281.

Angelo, T. "Doing Assessment As If Learning Matters Most." *AAHE Bulletin,* 1999, *51*(9), 3–6.

Argyris, C. "Teaching Smart People How to Learn." *Harvard Business Review,* 1991, *69,* 99–109.

Association of Governance Boards of Universities and Colleges. "Ten Public Policy Issues for Higher Education in 1999 and 2000." Washington, D.C.: Association of Governance Boards of Universities and Colleges, 2000. [http://www.agb.org /topten.cfm].

Berquist, W. H. *The Four Cultures of the Academy.* San Francisco: Jossey-Bass, 1996.

Biglan, A. "The Characteristics of Subject Matter in Different Disciplines." *Journal of Applied Psychology.* 1973, *57,* 195–203.

Birnbaum, R. "The Latent Organizational Functions of the Academic Senate: Why Senates Do Not Work But Will Not Go Away." *Journal of Higher Education,* 1989, *60*(4), 423–443.

Birnbaum, R. *How Colleges Work.* San Francisco: Jossey-Bass, 1991.

Clark, B. "Faculty Culture." In T. Lunsford (ed.), *The Study of Campus Cultures.* Boulder, Colo.: Western Interstate Commission on Higher Education, 1963.

Clark, B. *The Higher Education System: Academic Organization in Cross-National Perspective.* Berkeley: University of California Press, 1983.

Clark, B. "The Academic Life: Small Worlds, Different Worlds." *Educational Researcher,* 1989, June–July, pp. 4–8.

Garvin, D. "Building a Learning Organization." *Harvard Business Review,* 1993, *71,* 78–91.

Heifetz, R. *Leadership Without Easy Answers.* Cambridge, Mass.: Belknap Press of Harvard University Press, 1994.

Helgesen, S. *The Web of Inclusion: A New Architecture for Building Great Organizations.* New York: Doubleday, 1995.

Isabella, L. A. "Managing the Challenges of Trigger Events: The Mindsets of Governing Adaptation to Change." *Business Horizons.* 1992, *35,* 59–66.

Kuh, G., and Whitt, E. *The Invisible Tapestry: Culture in American Colleges and Universities.* ASHE-ERIC Higher Education Report No. 1. Washington, D.C.: Association for the Study of Higher Education, 1988.

Lenington, R. *Managing Higher Education as a Business.* Phoenix, Ariz.: American Council on Education and Oryx Press, 1996.

Massy, W. F., Wilger, A. K., and Colbeck, C. "Overcoming 'Hallowed Collegiality.'" *Change,* 1994, *26,* 10–20.

Mintzberg, H. *The Rise and Fall of Strategic Planning.* New York: Free Press, 1994.

Napier, R., Sidle, C., and Sanaghan, P. *High Impact Tools and Activities for Strategic Planning.* New York: McGraw-Hill, 1998.

Payne, H. C. "Can or Should a College Teach Virtue?" *Liberal Education,* 1996, *82,* 18–25.

Ramaley, J. A. "The View from Vermont." [http://www.uvm.edu/president/index /~inagspeech.html]. Burlington, VT: University of Vermont, 1997.

Ramaley, J. A. "The Making of a Budget: Strategic Thinking at a Public Research University." *Vermont Connection: The Student Affairs Journal of the University of Vermont,* 1998, *19,* 8–15.

Senge, P. *The Fifth Discipline: The Art and Practice of the Learning Organization.* New York: Doubleday, 1990.

Swenk, J. "Planning Failures: Decision Cultural Clashes." *Review of Higher Education,* 1999, *23,* 1–21.

University of Vermont. "Self-Study Report." [http://www.uvm.edu/~provost/accreditation/]. Burlington: University of Vermont, 1999a.

University of Vermont. "Strategic Change Process." [http://www.uvm.edu/president /index.html]. Burlington: University of Vermont, 1999b.

University of Vermont. "Strategic Change Steering Group Report." [http://www.uvm .edu/president/index/ html] Burlington: University of Vermont, 2000.

Weick, K. "Educational Organizations as Loosely Coupled Systems." *Administrative Science Quarterly,* 1976, *21,* 1–19.

Weick, K. *The Social Psychology of Organizing.* (2nd ed.) Reading, Mass.: Addison-Wesley, 1979.

Wheatley, M. J. *Leadership and the New Science: Discovering Order in a Chaotic World.* (2nd ed.) San Francisco: Berrett-Koehler, 1999.

REBECCA R. MARTIN *is vice provost for learning and information technology and associate professor of educational leadership, University of Vermont.*

KATHLEEN MANNING *is associate professor of higher education and student affairs, University of Vermont.*

JUDITH A. RAMALEY *is president and professor of biology, University of Vermont.*

INDEX

Academic programs: accreditation self-study of, 32; quality dimensions of, 8; teacher education, 54–55

Academics: accreditation program roles of, 7, 32; and administrators, interaction of, 98–102; characteristics of administrators and, 96

Accountability movement, the: assessment and accreditation and, 15, 18, 111; and "dirty laundry" airing issues, 89–90, 91; and higher education data, 83, 88, 89–90, 91–92

Accreditation: federal standards for, 39–40; the five purposes of, 6; granting (or reaccreditation), 10; initiating programs of, 78; maintaining, 9; and public relations, 49–50, 83; purposes and processes, 6–11; reasons for assessment and, 14–15; schools of education lack of, 51; traditional roles of, 11, 50, 54

Accreditation process, the: five steps for, 7–8; incorporating outcomes into, 67–70; professional organizations affected by, example of, 69–70. See also Self-study process, the institutional

Accreditation standards. See Standards, accreditation

Accreditation and student outcomes assessment: convergence of, 5–6, 17–18, 67–70; two key questions about, 5–6

Accreditation systems: distance-education alternative, 39; five elements of a multidimensional, 6–7; introducing revisions in, 69, 71–72, 74–80; voluntary or mandatory, 11–12, 50

Accrediting agencies, recognized: adoption of standards by, 79; CHEA standards for, 73–74; cooperation among, 77–78; duties of ASPA member, 70–71; electronic institutional portfolios and response to, 89; eligibility for becoming, 81n.5; example of constituencies of, 69–70; government standards for, 68; nongovernmental review of, 73–74; recognition process for, 7, 68, 73–74; survey of specialized ASPA member,

74–80; U.S. Department of Education requirements for, 71–73, 81n.5. See also Regional accreditation associations, the

Adelman, C., 38, 46n.4

Administration, academic institution, 79; culture of, 96

Admissions counseling, on-line, 46n.6

Adult education. See Distance education (higher education)

Affective learning outcomes, 25, 27

Alpert, D., 98

Alverno College, 13, 30

American Association of Colleges, 13

American Association for Higher Education, 84

American Council on Pharmaceutical Education, 70

American Dental Association, Commission on Dental Accreditation, 75

American Veterinary Medical Association, 75, 76

Angelo, T., 105–106

Argyris, C., 96, 102–103

Arts accrediting agencies, 78, 79

Assessment: communicating the findings of, 16, 50, 83; cyclical plans for ongoing, 69; definition of, 15; electronic institutional portfolio effects on, 90–91; formative or summative, 15, 17, 27–28; levels of implementation of, 31; of need for standards revision, 75; overlapping and conflicting purposes of, 15; quantitative and qualitative, 28–29; selecting methods and measures for, 16; self-study of culture of, 30–32. See also Student outcomes assessment

Assessment web site. See Electronic institutional portfolios

Association of Deans of Land Grant Universities, 52

Association of Specialized and Professional Accreditors (ASPA), 76–77; Code of Good Practice, 70–71, 81n.1; survey of specialized accreditor members of, 74–80

Astin, A., 16

117

Back Issue/Subscription Order Form

Copy or detach and send to:
Jossey-Bass Inc., 350 Sansome Street, San Francisco CA 94104-1342

Call or fax toll free!
Phone 888-378-2537 6AM–5PM PST; Fax 800-605-2665

Back issues: Please send me the following issues at $24 each.
(Important: Please include series initials and issue number, such as HE90.)

1. HE _____

_____

_____

$ _____ Total for single issues

$ _____ Shipping charges (for single issues *only;* subscriptions are exempt
from shipping charges): Up to $30, add $5^{50} • $30^{01}–$50, add $6^{50}
$50^{01}–$75, add $8 • $75^{01}–$100, add $10 • $100^{01}–$150, add $12
Over $150, call for shipping charge.

Subscriptions   Please ❑ start   ❑ renew my subscription to *New Directions
for Higher Education* for the year _____ at the following rate:

U.S.	❑ Individual $59	❑ Institutional $114
Canada:	❑ Individual $59	❑ Institutional $154
All Others:	❑ Individual $83	❑ Institutional $188

$ _____ Total single issues and subscriptions (Add appropriate sales tax
for your state for single issue orders. No sales tax on U.S. subscriptions.
Canadian residents, add GST for subscriptions and single issues.)

❑ Payment enclosed (U.S. check or money order only)
❑ VISA, MC, AmEx, Discover Card # _____ Exp. date_____

Signature _____ Day phone _____
❑ Bill me (U.S. institutional orders only. Purchase order required.)
Purchase order #_____
Federal Tax ID 135593032   GST 89102-8052

Name _____

Address _____

_____

Phone_____ E-mail _____

For more information about Jossey-Bass, visit our Web site at:
www.josseybass.com   **PRIORITY CODE = ND1**

United States Postal Service

Statement of Ownership, Management, and Circulation

1. Publication Title	2. Publication Number	3. Filing Date
New Directions For Higher Education	0 2 7 1 _ 0 5 6 0	9/29/00

4. Issue Frequency	5. Number of Issues Published Annually	6. Annual Subscription Price
Quarterly	4	$59 — Individual $114 — Institution

7. Complete Mailing Address of Known Office of Publication *(Not printer) (Street, city, county, state, and ZIP+4)*
350 Sansome Street
San Francisco, CA 94104

Contact Person
Joe Schuman
Telephone
415-782-3232

8. Complete Mailing Address of Headquarters or General Business Office of Publisher *(Not printer)*
Same As Above

9. Full Names and Complete Mailing Addresses of Publisher, Editor, and Managing Editor *(Do not leave blank)*
Publisher *(Name and complete mailing address)*

Jossey-Bass, A Wiley Company
(Above Address)

Editor *(Name and complete mailing address)*
Martin Kramer
2807 Shasta Road
Berkeley, CA 94708-2011

Managing Editor *(Name and complete mailing address)*

None

10. Owner *(Do not leave blank. If the publication is owned by a corporation, give the name and address of the corporation immediately followed by the names and addresses of all stockholders owning or holding 1 percent or more of the total amount of stock. If not owned by a corporation, give the names and addresses of the individual owners. If owned by a partnership or other unincorporated firm, give its name and address as well as those of each individual owner. If the publication is published by a nonprofit organization, give its name and address.)*

Full Name	Complete Mailing Address
John Wiley & Sons Inc.	605 Third Avenue New York, NY 10158-0012

11. Known Bondholders, Mortgagees, and Other Security Holders Owning or Holding 1 Percent or More of Total Amount of Bonds, Mortgages, or Other Securities. If none, check box ➤ ☐ None

Full Name	Complete Mailing Address
Same As Above	Same As Above

12. Tax Status *(For completion by nonprofit organizations authorized to mail at nonprofit rates) (Check one)*
The purpose, function, and nonprofit status of this organization and the exempt status for federal income tax purposes:
☐ Has Not Changed During Preceding 12 Months
☐ Has Changed During Preceding 12 Months *(Publisher must submit explanation of change with this statement)*

PS Form 3526, October 1999   *(See Instructions on Reverse)*

---

13. Publication Title	14. Issue Date for Circulation Data Below
New Directions For Higher Education	Summer 2000

15.		Extent and Nature of Circulation	Average No. Copies Each Issue During Preceding 12 Months	No. Copies of Single Issue Published Nearest to Filing Date
a.		Total Number of Copies *(Net press run)*	1,851	1,889
b. Paid and/or Requested Circulation	(1)	Paid/Requested Outside-County Mail Subscriptions Stated on Form 3541. *(Include advertiser's proof and exchange copies)*	837	858
	(2)	Paid In-County Subscriptions Stated on Form 3541 *(Include advertiser's proof and exchange copies)*	0	0
	(3)	Sales Through Dealers and Carriers, Street Vendors, Counter Sales, and Other Non-USPS Paid Distribution	0	0
	(4)	Other Classes Mailed Through the USPS	0	0
c.		Total Paid and/or Requested Circulation *[Sum of 15b. (1), (2),(3),and (4)]* ➤	837	858
d. Free Distribution by Mail *(Samples, complimentary, and other free)*	(1)	Outside-County as Stated on Form 3541	1	0
	(2)	In-County as Stated on Form 3541	0	0
	(3)	Other Classes Mailed Through the USPS	0	0
e.		Free Distribution Outside the Mail *(Carriers or other means)*	82	84
f.		Total Free Distribution *(Sum of 15d. and 15e.)* ➤	83	84
g.		Total Distribution *(Sum of 15c. and 15f)* ➤	920	942
h.		Copies not Distributed	931	947
i.		Total *(Sum of 15g. and h.)* ➤	1,851	1,889
j.		Percent Paid and/or Requested Circulation *(15c. divided by 15g. times 100)*	91%	91%

16. Publication of Statement of Ownership
☒ Publication required. Will be printed in the __Winter 2000__ issue of this publication.   ☐ Publication not required.

17. Signature and Title of Editor, Publisher, Business Manager, or Owner
Susan E. Lewis
Susan E. Lewis
Vice President & Publisher - Periodicals
Date 9/29/00

I certify that all information furnished on this form is true and complete. I understand that anyone who furnishes false or misleading information on this form or who omits material or information requested on the form may be subject to criminal sanctions (including fines and imprisonment) and/or civil sanctions (including civil penalties).

Instructions to Publishers

1. Complete and file one copy of this form with your postmaster annually on or before October 1. Keep a copy of the completed form for your records.

2. In cases where the stockholder or security holder is a trustee, include in items 10 and 11 the name of the person or corporation for whom the trustee is acting. Also include the names and addresses of individuals who are stockholders who own or hold 1 percent or more of the total amount of bonds, mortgages, or other securities of the publishing corporation. In item 11, if none, check the box. Use blank sheets if more space is required.

3. Be sure to furnish all circulation information called for in item 15. Free circulation must be shown in items 15d, e, and f.

4. Item 15h., Copies not Distributed, must include (1) newsstand copies originally stated on Form 3541, and returned to the publisher, (2) estimated returns from news agents, and (3), copies for office use, leftovers, spoiled, and all other copies not distributed.

5. If the publication had Periodicals authorization as a general or requester publication, this Statement of Ownership, Management, and Circulation must be published; it must be printed in any issue in October or, if the publication is not published during October, the first issue printed after October.

6. In item 16, indicate the date of the issue in which this Statement of Ownership will be published.

7. Item 17 must be signed.

Failure to file or publish a statement of ownership may lead to suspension of Periodicals authorization.

PS Form 3526, October 1999 *(Reverse)*